Easter
from the
Back Side

Easter from the Back Side

J. ELLSWORTH KALAS

Abingdon Press
NASHVILLE

EASTER FROM THE BACK SIDE

Copyright © 2008 by Abingdon Press

This book is printed on acid-free paper.

Library of Congress Cataloging-in-Publication Data

Kalas, J. Ellsworth, 1923–
    Easter from the back side / J. Ellsworth Kalas.
      p. cm.
    ISBN 978-0-687-49079-0 (pbk. : alk. paper)
    1. Easter.   2. Bible—Criticism, interpretation, etc. I. Title.
    BV55.K35   2008
    242′.36—dc22

                           2008038454

11 12 13 14 15 16 17 — 10 9 8 7 6 5 4 3

MANUFACTURED IN THE UNITED STATES OF AMERICA

To those who have found Easter
and
those who are still seeking it.

CONTENTS

INTRODUCTION

*E*aster is too grand an occasion to be experienced adequately in a single day. Our ancestors in the faith realized this and over a period of time developed a season of preparation. We call that season *Lent*. For well over fifteen hundred years, Christians have used this period of roughly seven weeks to prepare their souls for Easter Day.

In several branches of the church, especially Roman Catholicism, the Lenten season has been seen as a period of fasting—particularly in giving up some food or some practice for the weeks of Lent. No doubt this pattern has been misused by some, but the intention is good, and its faithful practice has blessed millions over the centuries.

In more recent years, many Christians—mostly in Protestant bodies—have made Lent a special time of study and increased devotion. I encouraged such a pattern in the nearly forty years that I served as a parish pastor in The United Methodist Church. Thus, I found great pleasure in the invitation to write a book for general use during the Lenten season.

I was asked to approach Easter "from the back side," as I have approached a number of subjects over the past nearly twenty years. I have tried to do just that in the seven chapters that follow. I begin with the Garden of Eden and end in heaven, which seems to me to be a pretty good Lenten trip. I'm glad for the chance to have you join me for this journey. I pray that you will find it a season of deeper faith and of greater love for God, for others, and for the fullness of life.

J. Ellsworth Kalas

CHAPTER 1

Why We Need Easter

GENESIS 3:1-7, 22-24: Now the serpent was more crafty than any other wild animal that the LORD God had made. He said to the woman, "Did God say, 'You shall not eat from any tree in the garden'?" The woman said to the serpent, "We may eat of the fruit of the trees in the garden; but God said, 'You shall not eat of the fruit of the tree that is in the middle of the garden, nor shall you touch it, or you shall die.'" But the serpent said to the woman, "You will not die; for God knows that when you eat of it your eyes will be opened, and you will be like God, knowing good and evil." So when the woman saw that the tree was good for food, and that it was a delight to the eyes, and that the tree was to be desired to make one wise, she took of its fruit and ate; and she also gave some to her husband, who was with her, and he ate. Then the eyes of both were opened, and they knew that they were naked; and they sewed fig leaves together and made loincloths for themselves. . . .

Then the LORD God said, "See, the man has become like one of us, knowing good and evil; and now, he might reach out his hand and take also from the tree of life, and eat, and live forever"—therefore the LORD God sent him forth from the garden of Eden, to till the ground from which he was taken. He drove out the man; and at the east of the garden of Eden he placed the cherubim, and a sword flaming and turning to guard the way to the tree of life.

*E*aster is an *answer.* It is such a dramatic, earthshaking answer that for nearly twenty centuries, artists of every kind and quality have been trying to portray its significance. It has been celebrated in music, from country-western and bluegrass to symphonies, and in graphic art that ranges from children's crayon work posted on the refrigerator to hangings in most of the art museums of the Western world. Poets and playwrights have celebrated Easter's answer in untold thousands of documents—and of course, no one can begin to estimate the number of sermons preached on this theme over these passing centuries.

So, what's the question? If Easter is such a monumental *answer,* what's the *question?*

To answer that question, I'll have to take us all the way back to the beginning. I mean, *really* the beginning. I'll have to take us back to a kind of mythical place. Not mythical in the sense of being untrue, but mythical in the truest sense—that is, something so true that it's difficult to tell the story without entering areas of mystery and wonder, where ordinary language fails us.

The Bible tells us that once our world was like a garden, fresh from the hands of a loving Creator. Everything about it was ideal. In fact, it was so good that God, the ultimate critic, smiled and pronounced it *very good.* For example, you didn't have to worry about the need for herbicides, because nothing could be classified as a weed; everything grew where it belonged, without crowding out other expressions of beauty, usefulness, and singularity. The animals were not afraid of the humans, and the humans were not afraid of the animals. The relationship was so good that the humans served *in loco parentis* (Latin for "in the place of a parent") to the animals. Nor did the animals prey on one another. It was all just one big, happy family—the kind of family all of us wish our families could be, except that this family included all the inhabitants of the planet. And when you wanted to have a picnic, you didn't have to worry about rain, because the water simply rose up from the earth, like a wonderful underground irrigation system.

But, as you must have guessed by now, something went wrong. I mean, big-time wrong. And the problem came not through the weeds or some malfunction of the watering system and not through a controversy among the animals, but by way of the chief executive of the planet, the creature made in the image of the Creator and therefore the one responsible for oversight of the whole operation. Of course this figures, because if the problem had been with the animals or the plants or the watering system, the person in charge could have taken care of it. But when the problem was with the person in charge—well, you can see for yourself what a mess it was.

Here's how it happened. I should warn you in advance that it's a strange story, so you may have difficulty handling it. I should also warn you that the strangest part of the story is not that you can't imagine it, but that you've seen it so many times that it doesn't get to you the way it should. Not only have you *seen* this story, you've sometimes been an actor in it. Lots of times, in fact. This means that you should grasp the story quite easily, but instead, most of the time you miss it. That's part of what makes the story so strange.

It was like this. One day, in the midst of all this perfection, someone suggested to Adam and Eve (the roots of our family tree and the ones originally trusted with the care of the perfect place) that perhaps things weren't really as good as the Creator had told them. In a way, this visitor (a serpent, though he didn't slither about at the time) was suggesting that perfection could be improved upon; to do violence to language, that perfection could be made "more perfect."

I hate to tell you this, but Adam and Eve believed the serpent. (I repeat, he didn't slither in those days; he was really quite handsome and able to sell almost anything, else our ancestors wouldn't have bought his grammatical misstatement.) In doing so, they misused their unique human gift, the power of choice.

And worse still, as far as you and I are concerned, they let loose on our planet the deadly plague that theologians and philosophers and street-corner preachers call *sin*. And between you and me, probably our human race wouldn't have been especially upset about the plague, except for what it brought with it—that is, the *consequences* of sin. Unless our thinking has been changed by a quite decisive meeting with God, most of us seem to get rather comfortable with sin. Not with the sins of other people, mind you; other people's sins are almost always obnoxious. But as for our own sins, we learn to live with them, and we eventually come to feel that other people should be able to live with them, too. So we say, after engaging in one of our pet sins, "I'm just that way, you know. I've always had a rather sharp tongue. The people who know me best take it for granted." As my late, dear friend Bud Rhyand used to say, "Every person thinks his own fleas are gazelles."

So sin doesn't necessarily upset us too much, except as other people express it, and except when the sin gets so out of hand that it destroys our health, our career, our family, or our self-respect. Or (and this is a severe mercy) when our consciences become so sensitive that we see sin the way God sees it, as an illness so abhorrent and so contrary to the nature of what was meant to be a perfect universe that the consequences are just what one should expect from something so ultimately evil.

The most obvious of these consequences is *death*. God had warned Adam about this: "You may freely eat of every tree of the garden; but of the tree of the knowledge of good and evil you shall not eat, for in the day that you eat of it you shall die" (Genesis 2:16-17). It is a touch of ironic realism that the first recorded death is neither Adam nor Eve, but their second son, Abel, murdered by their first son, Cain. (See Genesis 4:1-16.) Thus Adam and Eve experience death in what is arguably its worst form—not in one's own death but in the death of a loved one. And more: the death came by a further act of sin, the sickness they had set loose in the world, in a form they could not have anticipated in their worst fears—one of their children destroying another.

After the death of Abel and the gracious replacement in the birth of Seth (see Genesis 4:25), the writer of Genesis is about to go on with our discomfiting human record in the story of the flood. But first this theological historian with the touch of a novelist interrupts the unfolding of his plot to give us a collection of obituaries (see Genesis 5). These death notices have a monotonous beat: each gives us the name of the person, how long he lived until the birth of a first son, then a report of how many more years he lived bearing "other sons and daughters," and always concluding with the words, "and he died."

It reminds me of a classic weekly radio program of the 1930s, *Time Marches On,* produced and sponsored by *Time* magazine. At a given point each week, an announcer with haunting, stentorian tones announced, "Last week death came, *as it must for all men,* to . . . ," after which the announcer read the obituaries of the several notable public personalities who had died since the previous week's program. The Genesis writer made the same point by his drumbeat recitation, but interrupted himself once with the unique exception of Enoch, who "walked with God" and "was no more, because God took him" (Genesis 5:21-24). Thus Enoch becomes the fragment of hope in a story that from sin's entrance plays in an insistent minor key.

So this was the problem. Sin had come into the world as the result of humanity's disobedience to God, and with sin, death had come. And death, of course, is the ultimate disaster. Not simply physical death itself, but the premonitions of death that physical death has brought into our human story. The journalist Alan Brien tells of interviewing Brendan Behan (1923–1964), the brilliant Irish author and political personality, as he lay seriously ill in Middlesex Hospital. "Brendan," Brien asked, "do you ever think about death?" Behan pulled himself up in his bed and shouted, "Think about death? . . . I'd rather be dead than think about death."[1]

There's rugged humor in Brendan Behan's answer, the kind of earthy humor typical of the man, but there is also some very earthy theology. Behan put his finger on the heart of the matter: the ugliest part of death as we humans know it is in the fact that we must live with it all our lives before we finally have to contend with it in the first-person singular. We live with death in those occasions when we lose someone we know and love, and we live with it in those hours when we *think* about it. No wonder, then, that Behan preferred to be dead than to think about death.

But we can't escape thinking about death, because death is part of our definition. We humans are *mortals*. I remind myself that my ninth-grade Latin teacher explained that the word *mortal* comes from the Latin *mors mortis*—that is, the Latin term for "death." How painfully ironic that we humans have named ourselves by our inevitable end! Saint Augustine, next to the apostle Paul perhaps the greatest Christian theologian, once said that when a physician leans over the bed of a sick person, he may announce gravely, "He will die; he shall not get over this." But Augustine said that just as surely one might look into the crib on the first day of a baby's life and say, "She will die. She will not get over this."

Do I sound dreadfully negative? I really don't mean to; I mean only to describe our situation as it is. We are mortal creatures, so when one of us is born, there is only one thing we can say with certainty about that person's future: we know it will end in death. We don't know when, but we know it will come. Furthermore, we can never become so rich, so successful, or so powerful as to become an exception to this rule. John Donne, the brilliant seventeenth-century poet and preacher, dared to recognize that fact in a sermon he preached to the king of England at Whitehall. "What is so intricate, so entangling as death?" Donne asked rhetorically. "Whoever got out of a winding sheet?"[2] No one is so rich, so learned, or so powerful as to extract himself or herself from the death garment. And as the king had to realize as he listened to Donne's words, death is an equal-opportunity enemy; he indiscriminately oppresses rich and poor, famous and unknown, heroes and villains.

Our modern and postmodern world has remarkably reduced the physical pain of death, a fact for which all of us must surely be grateful. But it hasn't been as successful in delivering us from the fear of death. Several years ago, a British journalist said that we are now "secretly more terrified of death" than were the people of medieval times.[3] If so, I suspect it is partly because our ancestors lived closer to death than we do. Both births and deaths were likely to occur in the home, and sometimes they came so close together that the fragility of life and the inevitability of death were made dramatically clear. Perhaps, too, our fear of death is accentuated by the very fact that we have gained so much ground against our other enemies (such as physical pain), that the undiminished power of death is made all the more mysterious and all the more frightening.

Charles Wesley, who with his brother John founded the Christian renewal movement known as Methodism, left the world more than seven thousand hymns. A great many of them were autobiographical, reporting on Charles's own religious experience, but autobiographical also in describing the experience of the human race. In one of those hymns, written not long after the experience that transformed his life, Wesley described our human state and then the divine deliverance that followed:

> Long my imprisoned spirit lay,
>   fast bound in sin and nature's night;
> thine eye diffused a quickening ray;
>   I woke, the dungeon flamed with light;
> my chains fell off, my heart was free,
>   I rose, went forth, and followed thee.[4]

Wesley saw sin as an imprisonment of spirit that bound him, so that his soul dwelt, chained, in a dungeon. But the light of Christ broke into that dark and dank place, so that his chains fell off and his heart was free. John the Baptist had announced just such a possibility when he introduced Jesus by declaring, "Here is the Lamb of God who takes away the sin of the world!" (John 1:29).

But there had to be more to the story. It is a monumental thought that Jesus died for our sins, an expression of divine love beyond our comprehension. But if the story ended with Jesus' death, it would seem that sin had still won, since death had taken Jesus, too. Indeed, in a sense, if the story had ended with Jesus' death, sin's victory would have seemed greater than ever, in winning out over even the Christ of God.

That's where Easter comes in. The resurrection of our Lord is heaven's announcement that not only has the power of sin been broken, so too has the power of death. Michael Green, for many years the rector at Saint Aldate's Anglican Church in Oxford, England, said that death—"that final curb on freedom"—itself "suffered a death blow through the resurrection of Jesus."[5]

What happened so long ago, when our human race first used its power of choice to go against God rather than to go with God, was monstrous, indeed. It is not simply that someone once sinned but that all of us since then have followed the same irrational pattern. We live in the midst of the luxury of God's love, a luxury that shows itself in each breath we take, yet we choose to scorn that love. We live daily with the evidence that good is better than evil, yet we cast our vote so often for that which is shoddy and self-destructive. To put it baldly and yet somewhat philosophically, we seem to vote daily for death. No wonder, then, that death awaits us, and no wonder that we fear it, yet seem unable to escape it. The death penalty is all around us.

But our Lord Christ came, and with his death and resurrection he set free "those who all their lives were held in slavery by the fear of death" (Hebrews 2:15). So Charles Wesley, in another of the hymns following soon after his transforming religious experience, wrote, "Love's redeeming work is done . . . / Fought the fight, the battle won . . . / Death in vain forbids him rise . . . / Christ has opened paradise." And with such a grand message, no wonder Wesley chose to punctuate each statement with his *Alleluia!*[6]

This was the victory that we call Easter. It was the answer to our most insistent, most perplexing, and most hopeless question: what can be done about death? And because of that victory, as we move into the deep assurance of Christian faith, we are delivered from the plaguing specter, the fear of death. Mind you, we cannot help missing those who are taken from us by death. And neither are we likely to court death, because our very sense of the wonder of life makes us cherish it until we can enter life eternal. But the irrational fear is gone. Thomas Ken, the seventeenth-century poet, said it perfectly in what is one of the loveliest evening hymns: "Teach me to live, that I may dread / the grave as little as my bed."[7]

Why not, if the power of sin and death has been broken? G. A. Studdert-Kennedy, the extraordinary Anglican priest of the early twentieth century, saw death up close and often on the battlefields of World War I. But he wrote,

> So I looked up to God,
> And while I held my breath
> I saw Him slowly nod,
> And knew—as I had never known aught else,
> With certainty sublime and passionate,
> Shot through and through
> With sheer, unutterable bliss
> I knew—There was no death but this
> God's kiss.
> And then, the waking to an everlasting love.[8]

NOTES

1. Margaret Pepper, ed., *The Harper Religious and Inspirational Quotation Companion* (New York: Harper & Row, 1989), 130.

2. Ibid., 132.

3. Ibid., 139.

4. Charles Wesley, "And Can It Be that I Should Gain," 1739.

5. Michael Green, *Jesus Spells Freedom,* quoted in Margaret Pepper, *The Harper Religious & Inspirational Quotation Companion* (New York: Harper & Row, 1989), 133.

6. Charles Wesley, "Christ the Lord Is Risen Today," 1739.

7. Thomas Ken, "All Praise to Thee, My God, This Night," ca. 1674.

8. G. A. Studdert-Kennedy, "The Kiss of God," *World Theosophy Magazine,* June 1932, 417.

CHAPTER 2

Easter from an Ash Heap

JOB 19:13-27:
He has put my family far from
me,
and my acquaintances are
wholly estranged from me.
My relatives and my close
friends have failed me;
the guests in my house have
forgotten me;
my serving girls count me as a
stranger;
I have become an alien in
their eyes.
I call to my servant, but he gives
me no answer;
I must myself plead with him.
My breath is repulsive to my
wife;
I am loathsome to my own
family.
Even young children despise
me;
when I rise, they talk against
me.

All my intimate friends abhor me,
and those whom I loved have
turned against me.
My bones cling to my skin and
to my flesh,
and I have escaped by the
skin of my teeth.
Have pity on me, have pity on
me, O you my friends,
for the hand of God has
touched me!
Why do you, like God, pursue
me,
never satisfied with my flesh?
O that my words were written
down!
O that they were inscribed in
a book!
O that with an iron pen and
with lead
they were engraved on a rock
forever!
For I know that my Redeemer
lives,

and that at the last he will
    stand upon the earth;
and after my skin has been thus
    destroyed,
then in my flesh I shall see God,

whom I shall see on my side,
    and my eyes shall behold, and
    not another.
My heart faints within me!

*I*f Easter is true, our human race should have caught some glimmers of its dawn before the Son rose that morning in the garden near Golgotha. The truths that matter most to our human race have always whispered themselves into our consciousness long before their full announcement has been heard. This is so whether the issue is the dignity of the human race, the nature of God, the worth of the individual, or the grand fact and victory of Easter. Often that whisper comes somewhere in our earnest searching, because God is always attentive to our human hunger. Sometimes, surely, it comes when someone is at prayer or at some tentative groping in life's darkness. But sometimes the whisper breaks forth as a surprising declaration of faith and trust, right in the midst of a desert of hopelessness.

In my judgment, the greatest pre-Easter announcement was just such a declaration in the midst of hopelessness, and it came from an ash heap. It was a literal ash heap, in a sense all that was left of what had once been a proud fortune. But it was also an ash heap of despair, a place of burned-out hopes and of dreams that now seemed absurd.

Let me tell you the story. Much of it may be familiar to you, but we need to trace its details if we are to appreciate the dramatic words when suddenly they appear. Because as you know, the significance of what we say depends on the conditions in which we speak. "For better or worse" sounds beautiful at the altar of marriage; the phrase gets its integrity, however, when a marriage is at one of those "worse" places. So, too, it is quite idyllic when someone says in a blaze of sunlight that he believes in life beyond the grave, but the words have a more exquisite significance when they are spoken into the very teeth of darkness.

There was once, so the story goes, a man named Job. He was "the greatest of all the people of the east," not simply because of his extraordinary wealth and his standing in the community, but more particularly because he was "blameless and upright, one who feared God and turned away from evil" (Job 1:1, 3). I see him as a kind of model citizen, successful in both achievement and character, the kind of person whom parents point out to their children as someone to be admired and, if possible, replicated. And because of Job's success, people were inclined to conclude that he was God's favorite, too.

Then, suddenly and inexplicably, Job's world crashed. It was as if a tsunami of combined disasters settled in on this one human being. The biblical writer tells the story of Job's disasters by way of a series of messengers, each messenger identifying himself by the phrase, "I alone have escaped to tell you" (Job 1:15, 16, 17, 19). It was as if some malignant fate were purposely withholding one person from each disaster so there would be a messenger to deliver the wrenching news to its ultimate victim, Job. First, Job's (literal) stock holdings were wiped out in three sweeps of misery; and then—worst of all—his seven sons and three daughters, the fervent point of his prayers, were killed by an act of nature, "a great wind [that] came across the desert" (1:19).

At that point in Job's cosmic maelstrom, he tore his robe and shaved his head—acts of penitence and self-debasement— and "fell on the ground and worshiped" (1:20). Most of us stand in awe at this scene, marveling at the virtue of this remarkable person. Instead of railing against God and his circumstances, Job bowed in *worship*.

Now it would seem that nothing more could happen to Job. Instead, Job's disaster became, if possible, even more intimate: "loathsome sores" came upon his body, "from the sole of his foot to the crown of his head" (2:7). Perhaps a specialist in psychosomatic medicine would say that these physical eruptions were nothing other than Job's body reacting to the pain of his soul. At this place of misery, Job chose to treat his brokenness with brokenness. He "sat among the ashes" and scraped the discharge from his sores with a potsherd, a broken fragment of what had been a serving dish in better days (2:8). We aren't told why Job chose to sit among the ashes. Very possibly he was driven there by his wife and his few remaining servants, fearful of contamination from Job's pustulant sores. Or perhaps a place of ashes just seemed to Job to be the only appropriate place for someone so obviously rejected by life. So, too, with the potsherd. There is no hint in the story that the disasters had taken from Job his home or its furnishings, so Job might well have found a better instrument of cleansing. But I see Job as a poet of the soul, who chooses a throwaway object to tend his throwaway life. But if you think Job has nothing more to lose, I must tell you otherwise. His wife counsels him to be done with his admirable integrity: "Curse God, and die," she said (2:9). I think well of Job's wife. I see her as a good woman, who can't bear to see her husband suffer still more. And I suspect that she is at the end of her rope, too; after all, she as well as Job has lost the comfortable life of the well-to-do, and the children of her womb. Now I think she reasons, *Why should I watch this good and godly man waste into ugly disgrace?* But however well-meaning the counsel of Job's wife, Job has now lost her emotional and spiritual support. Her compassion itself becomes another drumbeat of hopelessness.

Still more pain is on the way. Job is about to lose his last tie to his grand and honored past, the trust of friends who had held him in unparalleled esteem. They come as a trio of self-ordained wisdom, with a fourth member who isn't mentioned until, late in their visit, he breaks silence.

They mean well. They intend to be true friends, but like many of us misled souls, they think Job needs advice when he really needs a sympathetic ear or, better yet, a quartet of sympathetic ears. To their credit, they sit in silence for seven days. Then, unable to contain their wisdom and their explanations any longer, they tell Job how it is that he has come to experience such disaster. Their answer is quite simple: he's suffering because he deserves it. The visiting contingent looks at Job's unspeakable misery and tells him he has it coming to him. If in some time of great grief you have been counseled by such a friend, may God in mercy give you strength. If, on the other hand, you have extended such counsel to another person in distress, may God forgive you.

Most of the body of the book of Job is made up of a running dialogue between Job and these friends, as the friends try to convince Job that if he hadn't done wrong, he wouldn't be in his present state, and Job insists on his innocence. Each contributor speaks eloquently, making his case in some of the most memorable speeches to be found anywhere in all of literature. They speak with passion and conviction. Job meets them point for point, with eloquence that if anything surpasses theirs. But Job senses that his ultimate argument is not with these friends but with God. In one especially moving speech, he declares that if only someone could get him an audience with God—a really fair hearing—he could make a case that the Almighty would have to consider.

In the midst of what may be Job's darkest hour his Easter vision breaks through. Beaten by repeated attacks from his friends, Job appeals piteously, "How long will you torment me, / and break me in pieces with words?" (19:1). He confesses that perhaps it is true that he has erred, but he asks his friends to see that God has become his enemy:

> He breaks me down on every side, and I am gone,
>   he has uprooted my hope like a tree.
> He has kindled his wrath against me,
>   and counts me as his adversary. (19:10-11)

And with that, Job begins an inventory of his absolute bankruptcy. Family? They are far from him. We learn near the end of the book that Job had brothers and sisters (see 42:11), but there is no sign of them at this point when family is most needed. We can only conclude that, seeing their brother's calamities, Job's siblings carefully absented themselves. As for acquaintances, they are "wholly estranged" (19:13), and people who were once guests in Job's house have now "forgotten" him (19:15). Job lived in a culture where servants were often the most loyal of associates. Not now; his servant girls count him as a stranger, and when Job calls to a servant, "he gives me no answer" (19:15-16). And Job is doing more than exercising the picturesque language of poetry when he cries, "My breath is repulsive to my wife; / I am loathsome to my own family" (19:17). Job's head-to-foot sores may have filled his mouth as well, making his breath rancid, and the very sight of his pus-ridden body would make even the most loving turn their eyes away. Indeed, I wonder to what degree the appearance of Job's body fed into the harsh language of Job's friends. I'm quite sure that the repulsion the friends felt at the sight of Job's body gave force to their philosophical judgments.

Little children can sometimes be remarkably blind to ugliness that repels adults. Not so in Job's case: "Even young children despise me" (19:18). Now Job looks at the committee of friends—people who have held him in such regard that they have come a distance to see him, and who care about him enough that they will, at the least, take the time to argue with him and condemn him—and he says, "All my intimate friends abhor me, / and those whom I loved have turned against me" (19:19).

And with that, Job makes an arms-stretched-out, exhausted body-and-soul appeal:

> Have pity on me, have pity on me, O you my friends,
>   for the hand of God has touched me!
> Why do you, like God, pursue me,
>   never satisfied with my flesh? (19:21-22)

It is just here, at this depth of lostness, where the ash heap itself has become an engulfing pit, that Job sees a ray of eternal hope, some astonishing glimpse of Easter victory. It comes to him with such power that he declares his confidence in the face of heaven and hell, of friends and foes, family and acquaintances. The poet and the prophet in Job unite in an appeal for writing instruments, so he can record what he is about to say. And no ordinary pen and ink will do. The wonder in his soul requires "an iron pen," so that his words can be "engraved on a rock forever!" (19:23-24). All of it so he can say this:

> For I know that my Redeemer lives,
>   and that at the last he will stand upon the earth;
> and after my skin has been thus destroyed,
>   then in my flesh I shall see God,
> whom I shall see on my side,
>   and my eyes shall behold, and not another.
> My heart faints within me! (19:25-27)

Let me pause first on that word *Redeemer*. It has particular roots in the Hebrew Scriptures. In the biblical law, the kinsman redeemer was one's next of kin, a person who because of that relationship had the responsibility to help in time of crisis—especially to buy back family property that (in our terms) was now about to suffer foreclosure, to avenge a robbery or a murder, and even to buy out of slavery someone who had lost freedom in the process of financial disasters. We see this law in action in the book of Ruth, when Boaz redeems the property of his kin, Naomi, and in the same act of responsibility, marries Ruth, the widow of Naomi's son. (In Boaz's case, he is actually the second of kin, but he takes on the responsibility when the next of kin refuses to do so.)

Who is in Job's mind when he declares that he knows that his Redeemer lives? Our translation capitalizes *Redeemer*, recognizing that for centuries this passage has been read by Christians as a reference to Jesus Christ. Thus Ephrem the Syrian, the fourth-century poet/theologian, wrote, "Here the blessed Job predicts the future manifestation of Emmanuel in the flesh at the end of time"; and John Chrysostom, the master preacher and bishop of Constantinople, also in the fourth century, asked, "Did Job know the doctrine of resurrection?" and answered his own question, "I believe so."[1]

It seems clear that Job is describing a more-than-human kinsman redeemer. He has already told us that his blood kin "have failed" him (19:14); besides, even if they were willing, they were unequipped to meet Job's need. He is looking beyond them to someone who "*at the last . . .* will stand upon the earth" (19:25, italics author's). Job anticipates some far-off but ultimate answer and justification. Indeed, he is content in the knowledge that it may be so far off that his "skin has been thus destroyed" (19:26). No matter; nevertheless, "in my flesh I shall see God" (verse 26). Job's testimony about his body is against all odds. His body, sore-possessed, pus-ridden, hardly looks worth saving. He senses that in time his "skin" will be destroyed—a logical conclusion, in light of its state at the moment of his speaking. Nevertheless, "*in my flesh* I shall see God."

Job realizes that this Redeemer is, indeed, *God.* More than that, Job knows that God is "on my side" and that when he sees God, he knows that it is "not another" that his eyes are beholding. And he knows that God sees value in his ash-heap body. As Job completes his statement, the emotional impact is so great that he adds, "My heart faints within me!" (19:27). His soul is suffering the exhaustion at the end of a spiritual marathon. In truth, Job's race is not yet over, but as far as he is concerned, the issue is settled. If I may say so, Job's experience is something like that of the disciples who experienced the resurrection of our Lord but nevertheless had to go on living in a world where the full impact of the Resurrection is yet to be fulfilled.

What did Job mean by his witness? Was he speaking specifically of the resurrection of Jesus Christ, and of the promise of our eventual resurrection, as Ephrem and Chrysostom and most of the church have believed for most of its history? Personally, I cast my vote with these centuries of believers. Did Job understand what he was saying? Personally, I think not. I believe that he *saw* more than he understood, and that his vision exceeded his comprehension.

Rowan Williams, the Archbishop of Canterbury, writes, "The resurrection is about God's commitment to this world of flesh and blood."[2] Job received his vision at just such a level. His personal world of flesh and blood was at its nadir. But with everything lost—family, wealth, community standing, health of body, friendship—Job somehow grasped the zenith. In the face of nothing, he found himself possessing everything. He was so sure of life and of bodily restoration, and of God's being on his side, that he couldn't restrain himself; he had to declare his faith and to plead for an instrument of recording that would sustain his certainty for the ages.

Many, many centuries later the church—basing its language on the story of Christ's resurrection and the apostle Paul's reporting—said in its creed, "I believe in the resurrection of the *body*."

Job said it first, from an ash heap.

NOTES

1. Thomas C. Oden, general ed., *Ancient Christian Commentary on Scripture*, vol. 6 of Old Testament (Downers Grove, Ill.: InterVarsity Press, 2006), 105–6.

2. Rowan Williams, *A Ray of Darkness* (Cambridge, Mass.: Cowley, 1995), 69.

CHAPTER 3

Easter for the Disillusioned

ECCLESIASTES 2:14-26:
The wise have eyes in their
  head,
  but fools walk in darkness.
Yet I perceived that the same
fate befalls all of them. Then I
said to myself, "What happens to
the fool will happen to me also;
why then have I been so very
wise?" And I said to myself that
this also is vanity. For there is no
enduring remembrance of the
wise or of fools, seeing that in the
days to come all will have been
long forgotten. How can the wise
die just like fools? So I hated life,
because what is done under the
sun was grievous to me; for all is
vanity and a chasing after wind.

I hated all my toil in which I
had toiled under the sun, seeing
that I must leave it to those who
come after me—and who knows
whether they will be wise or foolish? Yet they will be master of all
for which I toiled and used my
wisdom under the sun. This also
is vanity. So I turned and gave my
heart up to despair concerning
all the toil of my labors under
the sun, because sometimes one
who has toiled with wisdom and
knowledge and skill must leave
all to be enjoyed by another who
did not toil for it. This also is vanity and a great evil. What do mortals get from all the toil and
strain with which they toil under
the sun? For all their days are full
of pain, and their work is a vexa-
tion; even at night their minds
do not rest. This also is vanity.

There is nothing better for
mortals than to eat and drink,
and find enjoyment in their toil.
This also, I saw, is from the hand
of God; for apart from him who
can eat or who can have enjoyment? For to the one who
pleases him God gives wisdom

and knowledge and joy; but to the sinner he gives the work of gathering and heaping, only to give to one who pleases God. This also is vanity and a chasing after wind.

*I*should confess at the outset that each time I set out to read the book of Ecclesiastes, I have to persuade myself to like the writer of the book. I report this in the spirit of what the law calls "full disclosure." I reason that you have a right to know the prejudice with which I begin this chapter. Daphne Merkin, the novelist and literary critic, says that Ecclesiastes "opens with a great sputter of protest, an exhaust fume of indignation."[1] My own picture is less dramatic and perhaps even less generous than Ms. Merkin's: I see a spoiled teenager sitting in the midst of his sea of toys, complaining that none of them satisfy him—and worse yet, this teenager is in late middle age.

Yet, having said all of that, I feel sorry for this man. And in some ways I feel a kinship with him, partly because his is an affliction that troubles most humans, and also because you and I live in a generation that knows all too much about the too-many-toys syndrome. If any generation in history should have empathy for the writer of Ecclesiastes, it is ours—for those of us in the Western world, that is.

More than that, I know that what this man needs—indeed, he all but announces it, though without having the word for it—is the message of Easter. Someone has said that the book this man has given us has "the smell of the tomb about it." If so, Ecclesiastes is a perfect challenge for a book that chooses to look at Easter from the back side, and that wants to remind us that the tomb is not the end of the story.

Thus far I've been referring to this man anonymously. The fact is, his name is never specifically given, and the author himself is in some measure a matter of speculation. He identifies himself as a "Teacher" and as "the son of David, king in Jerusalem" (Ecclesiastes 1:1); and he tells us that these ruminations developed when he was "king over Israel in

Jerusalem" (1:12). He also tells us that he "became great and surpassed all who were before me in Jerusalem; also my wisdom remained with me" (2:9). From all these comments, there has been general agreement that the author was Solomon, the son of David who immediately succeeded him as king of Israel—the person often referred to as the wisest man who ever lived.

But many scholars for the past half century or more have pointed out that the Hebrew forms and grammatical features used in this book reflect a time several centuries later than Solomon's time. Therefore they opt for some unknown author who seeks simply to reflect what he perceives to be Solomon's thinking. It is on this basis that they refer to the author as *Qoheleth*, the Hebrew word for "Teacher" (or perhaps "Preacher"), by which the author refers to himself in the opening verse of the book.

But whether the author was King Solomon or some later person expressing what he sees as Solomon's sense of philosophical frustration, one thing is very clear: the author wrestles feverishly and somewhat pathetically with what he sees as the vanity of life. Thirty-eight times in this short book he tells us, in one way or another, that all is vanity—that is, literally, that life is a "breath" or a "vapor." That is, the feeling that you think you have something, only to see it dissolve in your hand; or more precisely, it dissolves in your hand without your seeing it do so, which makes its departure all the more mysterious, and thus accentuates the meaninglessness of it all.

Now if Ecclesiastes had been written by someone whose dreams had never been fulfilled, we would find it easier to dispose of his story. If he was the person who dreamed of being a class officer but never was nominated, who pictured election to Phi Beta Kappa but averaged a C in all subjects, who envisioned standing on the center step at the Olympic presentations but couldn't make a high-school track team—well, then, we'd understand this writer's frustration.

But he is at pains to tell us that in his life all of a person's ordinary dreams have come true. Indeed, only a person who had lived life on a broad stage could have imagined the favors that came to this man. When I thank God that my junior-high-school dreams have been fulfilled and that I have enjoyed blessings I didn't know existed, I am not only thanking God for dreams fulfilled, I am also confessing that my childhood dream base was probably rather modest. Not this man. He says that he was King David's son, which is to say that he had some inherently high expectations before he even left his mother's womb.

Well, this frustrated soul makes clear that he has had it all, but nothing he has experienced has satisfied his deepest, innermost longing. One of his first pursuits shows that he was not the spoiled child I've portrayed him to be: he tried hard labor, or at least observed those who do, and called it "all that curse of busy toil which God has given to the sons of Adam for their task." He concluded that "it was but frustration and lost labour, all of it" (1:14-15 Ronald Knox translation). As for those of us who honor learning and wisdom, Qoheleth says, "much wisdom, much woe; who adds to learning, adds to the load we bear" (1:18 Knox).

He was a person who gave full rein to his desires, including wine, spacious gardens to satisfy his love of nature, "singers, both men and women," silver and gold for sheer opulence, concubines for sensual excitement (2:3-8)—well, you get the idea; he tried everything. Robert Louis Stevenson said, "The world is so full of a number of things, / I'm sure we should all be as happy as kings." Well, this king (Solomon?) had it all, and it's clear that he wasn't very happy. And this is a special word for our postmodern culture, where the marvels of travel, endless restaurants, and iPod offer new experiences every day: "there is nothing new under the sun" (1:9). I think this wise man would tell us that the best we can hope for is some rather trivial, some quite transient (even if temporarily impressive) variation on the past.

So the king turns desperate. Ronald Knox's translation is sad but restrained: "Thus I became weary of life itself" (2:17); the New Revised Standard Version puts it more harshly: "So I hated life."

What drives this person? Is he simply a spoiled, over-indulged rich man, or is there more to him than that? After all, he has enough learning and enough innate culture to give us what Alfred Lord Tennyson called "the greatest poem of ancient or modern times," so he's more than just a disgruntled misanthrope or a grouchy old man. Why does this man who has so much—part of it inherited but also much of it the achievement of his own disciplined effort and his own brilliant mind—look back on his life at a vantage point of what we might call late middle age and find that he hates life?

One thing that bothers him is the prospect that after he dies, his wealth (including what we today might call his art collection and his accumulation of antiques) will be squandered by those who inherit it. "An heir," he cries, "would he be wise man or fool? None could tell; but his would be the possession of all I had toiled for so hard, schemed for so anxiously; could there be frustration worse than this?" (2:19 Knox). All of us can sympathize with this fear. We've read newspaper accounts of how some second and third generations of descendants of the very wealthy spend their inheritance in absurd and profligate ways. Or closer to home, we think of friends who look at some beloved collection of books or pewter or family heirlooms and worry how their cherished items will be treated after their death. For some, the thought of careless disposal is a kind of personal sacrilege, a scorning of their love. Yes, the writer has a point.

Also, this man is troubled by injustice, and he fears much of it will never be made right: "Moreover I saw under the sun that in the place of justice, wickedness was there"; and he hopes that God will make it all right someday, but he doubts it: "For the fate of humans and the fate of animals is the same; as one dies, so dies the other" (3:16, 19). So he concludes that it makes no difference how we live, because who can say if ever justice will be done? He is certain that life often works out negatively on this earth: "There is a vanity that takes place on earth, that there are righteous people who are treated according to the conduct of the wicked, and there are wicked people who are treated according to the conduct of the righteous. I said that this also is vanity" (8:14). Most of us have known times when we'd say *Amen* to that statement. We've known instances when we've said that life isn't fair; that phrase may have become a mantra for some of us, so much so that when some less jaded soul has complained that life isn't fair, we've answered, "Whatever made you think that it should be?" Perhaps sometimes our thinking is closer to Solomon's than we want to acknowledge.

But I think the greatest problem for this man—the problem that in reality encompasses all the others—is the feeling that this world is the end of it all. His only sense of immortality is in being remembered, and he senses that in time everyone is forgotten. The brilliant twentieth-century philosopher-theologian Paul Tillich said, "In the depth of the anxiety of having to die is the anxiety of being eternally forgotten."[2] That is, Professor Tillich reasoned, it isn't death itself that threatens us so deeply, but that we will have no place in memory. All of us want to be remembered—and preferably, of course, to be remembered favorably. All of us have nodded agreement when in the play *Death of a Salesman*, the wife of Willy Loman pleads that even though Willy never accomplished a great deal, "He's a human being," so "attention must be finally paid."[3]

But while all of us want to be remembered by family and friends, and while many would hope to have some small page in history, I submit that in Tillich's sentence the key word is *eternally*. We want some remembrance on this planet, but we want more than that. Something in us wants to be remembered longer. Much, much longer. We want to be remembered *eternally*. Which is to say that while it is normal and worthy to want a place in the memory of our fellow humans, something in us wants a place in memory quite beyond that. We want to be remembered by God. We want a toehold in eternity.

We humans sense that there ought to be Someone, somewhere, who cares about us enough that we will have a place in that Person's memory. The instinct within us of our own worth beyond this planet compels us to long for that promised eternity and for recognition by the One who inhabits, empowers, and assures that eternity.

At this point I am forced to revise my thinking about this ancient poet-philosopher—and, in fact, to apologize to him. Instead of criticizing him for being dissatisfied with all he has, I should give him credit for arguing that there should be more. I must give him credit for thinking beyond the boundaries that probably were taken for granted by most of his contemporaries. That is, I believe that there is in every person this intimation of eternity, but I suspect that a great many of the people with whom Solomon (if I may call him that) associated had gradually made peace with their finer longings, pushing them aside in order to go on with life as it is.

It is sometimes said that Ecclesiastes is the most modern book in the Bible. Certainly it can be argued that never before has there been a generation in which so many people—including even many of those living within the official definition of *poverty*—have so many sensory benefits so easily available. And yet these benefits haven't brought commensurate happiness. Some analysts say that instead the increased favors have raised our expectations. We begin with some definition of happiness ("If only I can get . . . be . . . own such and such"), only to discover when we win that place or prize that in time we want something more. In the language of what was once a prize-winning popular song, "Is that all there is?"

Solomon can't make peace with the idea that there is no more. He wrestles desperately:

> I said in my heart with regard to human beings that God is testing them to show that they are but animals. For the fate of humans and the fate of animals is the same; as one dies, so dies the other. They all have the same breath, and humans have no advantage over the animals; for all is vanity. . . . Who knows whether the human spirit goes upward and the spirit of animals goes downward to the earth? (3:18-19, 21)

Solomon fears—to put it in the language of some modern cynic—that we are all nothing more than creatures on our way to becoming fertilizer, but he simply cannot make peace with that idea. Where Job strains from his ash heap with a cry of faith, Solomon shakes his head and says, "I must do more research. But for now, the answer seems to be vanity."

The Teacher/Preacher concludes his book on a faith note, but a commonsense faith note. He counsels the young to remember their Creator "before the days of trouble come, and the years draw near when you will say, 'I have no pleasure in them' " (12:1)—the years, apparently, that he has reached. He makes a kind of apology for having written this book and for his own life of research: "Of making many books there is no end, and much study is a weariness of the flesh" (12:12). But for "the end of the matter," he offers this: "Fear God, and keep his commandments; for that is the whole duty of everyone. For God will bring every deed into judgment, including every secret thing, whether good or evil" (12:13-14).

This is a tempered answer, the sort one might expect from a scholar who has compiled all the hard data and gives a tentative conclusion. It is a very good one, mind you, for as far as it goes. Fear God and keep his commandments—this is everyone's duty. And leave the rest to God, who is the ultimate judge.

I am revising my earlier evaluation of this man. I honor him for struggling beyond what was no doubt the prevailing philosophy of his time, that the grave was the end of it all and that the best human beings could hope for was to leave something behind for their families and perhaps to be remembered for a generation or two. He wants something more than that, and he blusters that if there isn't something more, then it is all vanity.

I honor this Teacher and moral researcher for seeing the problem, for struggling for an answer, and for getting as far as he did. I see him as a researcher—a spiritual researcher, that is—who never finds the answer he's seeking. In his research he is like those hundreds of scientists who worked at the mystery of polio before Jonas Salk and Albert Sabin found the vaccine. The earlier researchers knew there had to be some solution, and they labored to find it. Salk and Sabin completed the journey. Solomon's faith was hidden under a burden of disappointment and near hopelessness, but he insisted there ought to be something more. It just didn't make sense to him that this was all there is—no matter how much "this" might be. He saw Easter from the back side. I'm sorry that he died without finding what he was seeking.

NOTES

1. Merkin, Daphne, "Ecclesiastes," in *Congregation: Contemproary Writers Read the Jewish Bible*, ed. David Rosenberg (New York: Harcourt Brace Jovanovich, 1987), 393.
2. Paul Tillich, *The Eternal Now*, quoted in Pepper, *The Harper Religious & Inspirational Quotation Companion*, 138.
3. Arthur Miller, *Death of a Salesman* (New York: Penguin, 1999), act 1.

CHAPTER 4

Ezekiel Celebrates Easter

EZEKIEL 37:1-10: The hand of the LORD came upon me, and he brought me out by the spirit of the LORD and set me down in the middle of a valley; it was full of bones. He led me all around them; there were very many lying in the valley, and they were very dry. He said to me, "Mortal, can these bones live?" I answered, "O Lord GOD, you know." Then he said to me, "Prophesy to these bones, and say to them: O dry bones, hear the word of the LORD. Thus says the Lord GOD to these bones: I will cause breath to enter you, and you shall live. I will lay sinews on you, and will cause flesh to come upon you, and cover you with skin, and put breath in you, and you shall live; and you shall know that I am the LORD."

So I prophesied as I had been commanded; and as I prophesied, suddenly there was a noise, a rattling, and the bones came together, bone to its bone. I looked, and there were sinews on them, and flesh had come upon them, and skin had covered them; but there was no breath in them. Then he said to me, "Prophesy to the breath, prophesy, mortal, and say to the breath: Thus says the Lord GOD: Come from the four winds, O breath, and breathe upon these slain, that they may live." I prophesied as he commanded me, and the breath came into them, and they lived, and stood on their feet, a vast multitude.

*C*harles Dickens began his *Tale of Two Cities* with what are probably the most memorable opening lines of any novel in the English language: "It was the best of times, it was the worst of times . . ." The prophet Ezekiel, in his time, would have allowed no such equivocating. He didn't know too much about the best of times, but he knew that his times were bad, very bad; as bad, he might have contended, as human times could be. They were so bad, in fact, that Ezekiel had to take his majestic prophetic vision and the grandeur of his poetic language to their limits in order to find an adequate description. Elie Wiesel, whose Holocaust experience gives him credentials for judging such matters, says that no one but Ezekiel "had ever seen such darkness, the total darkness that precedes the break of dawn."[1]

Bear with me, then, while I tell you about Ezekiel and his times, so that you will understand with me the prophet's darkness and the break of dawn that followed—and how it was that in a strange and very different way, Ezekiel had an Easter experience of his own.

The nation of Judah—all that was left of what had once been the proud Israel of King David and King Solomon—entered a particularly dismal period in the mid-seventh century B.C. Judah was never really a power broker among the nations of the ancient Middle East. Often she seemed no more than a pawn to be used and abused by the dominant military powers. When Assyria flexed its muscles, carrying away the ten northern tribes of what had once been a twelve-tribe confederation, Judah sensed that she might be next to be consumed by the Assyrian armies. Thus Judah lived in constant peril of massive military invasions.

Most of Judah's kings didn't help matters. Manasseh had a long reign, but it was marked by much brutality and injustice, and the nation's religious life became more marginal as Manasseh led the people into practices that were far from God's law. The best thing to be said for Manasseh's son Amon was that his reign was so short. Then, however, there was a blessed faith-revival under King Josiah. But Josiah's later military decisions weakened the nation, and the kings who followed—several of very short duration—were exercises in ineptness and spiritual confusion. Eventually a new national power, the Babylonians, invaded Judah. At that point Ezekiel's ministry of prophecy came into play. I have given us a summary of the years preceding Ezekiel's time in order to help us see the long miasma of confusion, apostasy, and despair that set the emotional, political, and spiritual stage for Ezekiel's ministry.

As the Babylonians invaded Judah, they carried off many of the brightest and the best of the young men of the nation. In this the Babylonians were following a quite sophisticated political formula. They recognized that many of the people in the nations they conquered were superior scholars or craftsmen, so they strengthened their own arsenal of leadership with these people—much as a present-day conqueror might apprehend a nation's scientists and computer specialists.

Ezekiel was one of those taken captive in an early Babylonian military action. As far as we can tell, he spent all of his rather lengthy ministry as a prophet in exile, ministering at first to his fellow exiles but also in some fashion to the people of Judah who were still resident in the homeland. On the surface it seems that he wasn't notably successful with either group. Even the best prophet, the best political pragmatist, or the best crusader is limited to the material with which he works. Ezekiel's material was not promising. As I have already indicated, except for Josiah, Judah had been led for roughly a century by kings who were themselves either apostate or spiritually neutral. I cannot judge the quality of the appointed spiritual leaders of the time, the priests and Levites, but, as a matter of fact, it would have been very difficult in Israel or Judah for the general level of spirituality to rise much higher than that of the king. Because of Israel's history and the relationship between the nation's political and religious leaders, the king was a kind of inevitable spiritual arbiter.

I suppose I'm simply telling you that Ezekiel had a disheartening, enervating assignment. For the people who were still resident back in Judah, he was a distant voice, easily discounted. When Ezekiel counseled them not to immigrate to Egypt, I suspect that they reasoned that he had no business advising them from his detached location. As for his fellow exiles in Babylon, their energies had to be invested in simply staying alive and in calculating how to maintain a successful, conciliatory relationship with their captors.

But Ezekiel had a kind of spiritual toughness that kept him going. Spiritually, it can be argued that he came from good stock, since his father was a priest in Judah. Of course, this doesn't finally prove anything; all of us have known persons whose parents were good or godly people but who didn't follow such a course themselves; and indeed, all of us know that professional religious leaders don't necessarily live up to their title or calling. Still, the odds are reasonably good.

I am fascinated by the insights into Ezekiel's personality as revealed by his writing. In one instance, he seems the closest thing to a meticulous historian. Thirteen times in the course of his book he gives us the specific date on which he has received a particular vision. No other Hebrew prophet is so exact in such details. At another time, Ezekiel writes like an architect or an engineer as he lays out in almost painful detail a description of the temple he envisions as replacing the one that the Babylonians have destroyed. At still another time, Ezekiel sounds like a novelist as he describes his nation's spiritual apostasy in some of the most lurid sexual language to be found in the Bible. And then, of course, there is the writing for which he is best known—even among those who don't know the Bible particularly well—in which he describes his exotic visions.

Carl Gordon Howie says that Ezekiel "was not what we should consider a 'normal person,'" but that this "abnormality" itself is the "key to his greatness, as has been the case with many of history's notable personalities."[2] I submit that perhaps only such an irregular personality was sufficient for the times in which Ezekiel lived and the circumstances in which he ministered. The people to whom he preached were dull of spiritual hearing. He spoke with a shocking directness that was calculated to get their attention. Even if he could not with certainty win their souls, he would startle them into listening, so that at the least they would know that a prophet of the Lord had spoken to them. Mind you, they might not always have realized it at the time, but Ezekiel's dramatic, sometimes almost irrational challenges must eventually have had a cumulative power. They might not agree with him, but neither could they comfortably ignore him.

I should interrupt myself here with a question that may be nagging you. Why should Ezekiel be so upset over the state of his nation? Why should it bother him that some of his fellow citizens chose to abscond to Egypt rather than remain part of the larger body in Babylon? And why be upset that many in Babylon were choosing to accommodate themselves to a foreign culture; isn't it better to be a live dog than a dead lion? And if the dominant power is of such strength that there is no hope of gaining freedom, why not forget about the homeland and make a life for yourself in the foreign culture? Indeed, what's so bad about appreciating the culture of another people to the point that you adjust yourself to their way of living, celebrating, and thinking?

These are challenging, pragmatic questions, and history has been shaped by the way people have dealt with the alternatives these questions present. Take such a matter as *freedom*: is it worth the sacrifices some have made in order to achieve it? And *justice*: it's such a high-sounding word, but its price is sometimes unreasonably high. Is it better perhaps to lower one's expectations and to live with things as they are? Perhaps all those people who work and sacrifice for high causes are small-time Men and Women of La Mancha, tilting at windmills, while others have the good sense to accept life as it is, never dreaming too much, never worrying overmuch about the pain of other people, and never making themselves miserable for causes that are almost surely doomed to be lost.

I confess to you that even as I write the paragraphs I've just finished, I resent them. I resent giving them a place on paper, although I know that vast numbers of people live by such arguments—spoken, acknowledged, or not—every day. You see, I don't believe the Bible will allow us to reason as self-centeredly and as shortsightedly as I have just described. The Bible, both Old Testament and New, insists that we humans are made of better stuff, that something in us can never make peace with what is less than God's perfect will for our world.

And I believe that many great souls who have known little or nothing of the Scriptures have nevertheless had something of the same divine vision. I cannot fully explain this; perhaps the secret is hidden in the word spoken in John's Gospel, that Jesus Christ is the "true light, which enlightens everyone" (John 1:9). If indeed (as I believe), the light of Christ is at work in every human being, we can expect that even quite secular and quite pagan souls long for a better world—a longing that comes from beyond themselves and that may be inconsistent with other elements in their thinking or their personalities.

Nevertheless, those whose vision for such a world is deep enough that they will struggle to bring it to pass will always be a minority. The rest of the world pushes such feelings aside in the struggle to survive. Only a few, a very few, take on themselves the pain to work toward such an end. Ezekiel was such a person. And he paid for it. As Elie Wiesel puts it, "He was always suspected by everyone, resented for being on God's side, for knowing too much, for protesting against false prophets and false comfort. Whatever he predicted to others ultimately happened to him, too."[3] I suppose it is a kind of final indignity that Ezekiel was buried in Babylon, an exile even in his death. When the patriarch Joseph died, he asked that his bones eventually be carried to the land of his fathers, the land of promise, and centuries later when the children of Israel fled Egypt, they carried Joseph's bones with them (Genesis 50:24-25; Exodus 13:19). Ezekiel enjoyed no such corporeal exit.

But even in the midst of his rejections and persecution and in his long exile, Ezekiel had his moments. None was more sublime, I venture, than the day God took him to a cemetery. Ezekiel begins this story without any embellishments. Indeed, it is the only one of Ezekiel's visions that he does not date for us. Instead he begins simply, "The hand of the LORD came upon me, and he brought me out by the spirit of the LORD and set me down in the middle of a valley; it was full of bones" (37:1). I suspect that I gave unmerited dignity to this setting when I referred to it a moment ago as a "cemetery." It was, yes, a place of the dead, but not one chosen by the bereaved as a burial place for their beloved. At best it could have been seen as a battlefield where the corpses have been left to blanch in the sun. It could as well have been a place where bodies were thrown frantically during a plague. Whatever, there was no time for burial. This was a place of death, but without the benefit of structured grief or the rituals of remembrance. No stones here, with expressions of love or memory; just a valley "full of bones."

I see a playful quality in God, but you will laugh only if you have the faith to see the humor. Ezekiel reports that God "led me all around [the bones]; there were very many lying in the valley, and they were very dry" (37:2). Folks have sometimes shown me more of their hobby shop or their prize collection of railroad restroom signs than I wanted to see, so I empathize with Ezekiel on this trip. Five minutes in a valley of bones is enough already; the prophet hadn't hoped for an escorted tour. But God has a point to make in this fun trip; it's important for Ezekiel to know just how bad things are. And the prophet confesses that he's gotten the point: these bones, he now realizes, are *very dry*. Which is to say, things are about as bad as they can get.

Then God prods Ezekiel with a question: "Mortal, can these bones live?" And Ezekiel, God bless him, is ready with an answer: "O Lord GOD, you know" (37:3). The prophet is savvy enough to put the ball back in God's court.

God isn't finished being playful: "Prophesy to these bones, and say to them: O dry bones, hear the word of the LORD" (37:4). I've preached in a variety of places ranging from a street corner in skid row to cathedral-like churches where one ascends into a pulpit so lifted up that you're sure the cherubim and seraphim are within arm's reach, but I've never preached to a congregation altogether, unmistakably, mockingly dead. God seems to be inviting Ezekiel to put his call to the test: is he really an anointed prophet, or are there congregations beyond the reach of his talents?

Well, I won't hold you in suspense any longer. Ezekiel decided to do what God said, ridiculous as it might seem to do so, and as he preached, "there was a noise, a rattling, and the bones came together, bone to its bone" (37:7). By the time the prophet got to point three in his sermon, the bones "stood on their feet, a vast multitude" (37:10).

Now God told Ezekiel the point of this remarkable exercise. The bones represented his people, Israel, a people who said (with good reason, I would add), "Our hope is lost; we are cut off completely" (37:11). But God sees it differently: "I am going to open your graves, and bring you up from your graves, O my people; and I will bring you back to the land of Israel. And you shall know that I am the LORD, when I open your graves" (37:12-13).

This was God's message to a people who saw such a hopeless situation that it could be pictured only as a nation utterly dead; indeed, reduced to a boneyard, in which the bones were *very dry*. And worse, a good share of the people either didn't realize how bad the situation was or simply didn't care; they had learned to accommodate themselves to their hopeless state. But there was one man who cared, a son of a priest, a man who couldn't shake himself free of God's vision for Israel, and whose only reward for such a love and such a vision was the misery of unceasing despair. So God took that lonely soul on a peculiar journey. It was, at the first, a journey that seemed only to underline all of Ezekiel's worst analysis, as if God were saying, "You think things are bad? You have no idea how really bad they are." Then, at the most hopeless moment, God challenged Ezekiel to dare to prophesy—that is, to declare faith in the face of death—and as he did, the miracle of life began to assert itself, until at last the valley of bones became the playground of life.

This is a message for anyone who is living with a hopeless scene and who has the holy misfortune to want to see the situation redeemed. It may be a rundown life or a rundown neighborhood, a rusty family or a rusty city, an economy gone bust or a world apparently committed to self-destruction: the valley of dry bones has a panorama of faces. God is committed to life, so those who believe will dare to bring their death valleys to him.

The specific theme of Easter is the promise that through our Lord's resurrection, death has lost its sting and its victory. I believe that the extension of this truth applies to all those areas of our experience where death makes its insistent claims—war, poverty, prejudice, materialism. At any such place of death, the Easter faith fills our souls with the unconquerable conviction that Christ has won, and that to partake of his life is to become his ally in the unceasing battle against death, whatever its form. And to know, even as we struggle, prophesy, and pray, that the valley is never so dark and the bones never so dry that the battle is lost. God's Easter is always winning.

NOTES

1. Elie Wiesel, "Ezekiel," in *Congregation: Contemporary Writers Read the Jewish Bible*, ed. David Rosenberg (New York: Harcourt Brace Jovanovich, 1987), 167.

2. Carl G. Howie, *The Book of Ezekiel*, vol. 13 of The Layman's Bible Commentary (Richmond, Va.: John Knox Press, 1961), 15.

3. Wiesel, "Ezekiel," 177.

CHAPTER 5

Easter Is a Love Story

JOHN 20:1-18: Early on the first day of the week, while it was still dark, Mary Magdalene came to the tomb and saw that the stone had been removed from the tomb. So she ran and went to Simon Peter and the other disciple, the one whom Jesus loved, and said to them, "They have taken the Lord out of the tomb, and we do not know where they have laid him." Then Peter and the other disciple set out and went toward the tomb. The two were running together, but the other disciple outran Peter and reached the tomb first. He bent down to look in and saw the linen wrappings lying there, but he did not go in. Then Simon Peter came, following him, and went into the tomb. He saw the linen wrappings lying there, and the cloth that had been on Jesus' head, not lying with the linen wrappings but rolled up in a place by itself. Then the other disciple, who reached the tomb first, also went in, and he saw and believed; for as yet they did not understand the scripture, that he must rise from the dead. Then the disciples returned to their homes.

But Mary stood weeping outside the tomb. As she wept, she bent over to look into the tomb; and she saw two angels in white, sitting where the body of Jesus had been lying, one at the head and the other at the feet. They said to her, "Woman, why are you weeping?" She said to them, "They have taken away my Lord, and I do not know where they have laid him." When she had said this, she turned round and saw Jesus standing there, but she did not know that it was Jesus.

Jesus said to her, "Woman, why are you weeping? Whom are you looking for?" Supposing him to be the gardener, she said to him, "Sir, if you have carried him away, tell me where you have laid him, and I will take him away." Jesus said to her, "Mary!" She turned and said to him in Hebrew, "Rabbouni!" (which means Teacher). Jesus said to her, "Do not hold on to me, because I have not yet ascended to the Father. But go to my brothers and say to them, 'I am ascending to my Father and your Father, to my God and your God.'" Mary Magdalene went and announced to the disciples, "I have seen the Lord"; and she told them that he had said these things to her.

*E*aster is a love story. I learned this truth with repeated poignancy hundreds of times in the years that I was a pastor. Each time I stood at a graveside, speaking the solemn, rhythmic words, "Earth to earth, ashes to ashes, dust to dust," I would see something in the faces of the bereaved. People who previously might have shown little interest in the afterlife now had a personal stake in such a possibility. "I can't fully say that I believe in the world to come," a man said tentatively. "But I *want* to." Love was compelling him. What logic, metaphysics, or religion could not do, love could.

I see this quality at work in the first Easter story. When the Gospel writer tells us, "Early on the first day of the week, while it was still dark, Mary Magdalene came to the tomb" (John 20:1), I know that he is making a point by his emphatic references to the time of day. John's Gospel pays more attention to elements of time than any other New Testament book, so when he tells us that this event took place *early*, I know that this is no incidental detail to him. Indeed, even the word *early* is not sufficient to make his point; John underlines what he feels by telling us that "it was still dark." In a world where there were no streetlights and no flashlights, the time before the breaking of dawn could be so dark that every step was taken at hazard. If this woman, Mary, had been showing any common sense, she would have waited at least a little while longer before coming to the tomb. What difference would a few minutes make? After all, the body to which she and her friends were bringing burial spices was not going to go away; there really wasn't any reason to hurry.

Except, of course, that love compels one to hurry.

We know just enough about Mary Magdalene to give our imaginations an easy launching pad. We're told that she was one from whom Jesus had cast seven devils (see Mark 16:9). If you're a bit of a Bible student, you know that *seven* is the biblical number for completeness; whether for good or ill, seven is the total package. Whatever had been wrong with Mary, whatever the evil that possessed her, it had been so severe and so dramatic that it was as bad as it could get. And if your postmodern mind rejects the language of devils and demons, simply understand this, that at the least the biblical writer is telling us that this woman's personality was as fiercely torn and as utterly demolished as the writer could imagine. Those who knew Mary Magdalene best felt that her condition—whatever language you use to describe it—was as lost and as hopeless and as terrifying to observe as a human condition could be.

Our contemporaries (and for that matter, many in twenty previous centuries) are inclined to read Mary's story in sexual terms: they picture her as a woman who knew no moral restraints, giving her a kind of cheap glamour. Some imagine her to have been abused in her young girlhood and thus a victim; others see her as a person who longed passionately for love and who channeled all that longing into sexual activity. But any such interpretation is far too simple and perhaps too much of a projecting of our own hidden corners—and easy pickings, certainly, for a film or television scriptwriter to inhabit in our day, or for a novelist or poet to embody in any century.

But whether or not Mary's demons were sensual (and very possibly this was one element in her personality), her problem was more profound, more intense, and more frightening. Our usual portrayals of Mary are inclined to give her a seductive quality, someone whose innate attractiveness would be hard to resist. I expect that if we had seen her when first she came to Jesus, we would have seen, rather, a person we would seek to avoid: haunted eyes, a nervous, restless body, perhaps skeleton-like from what we now call anorexia; at times reaching out for friendship and then, without warning, roughly brushing aside any kindness or love. This was a woman so driven by her demons, without and within, that only a fool or a saint (or more particularly, the Son of God) would be inclined to love her.

She was the first to see our resurrected Lord.

I'm looking just now for a reason. I want to know why a certain person, or persons, came first to experience Easter. This is no idle curiosity. I tell myself that if you and I can know the secret that made such a person (or persons) first at the Easter miracle, perhaps then *we* will be able to experience Easter more deeply and with a greater measure of reality.

But I want to leave Mary for a moment so we can look at another person who was an early personality on that first Easter. When Mary found the tomb empty on her "still dark" visit, "she ran and went to Simon Peter and the other disciple, the one whom Jesus loved," and told them what she had found, a tomb from which someone (she thought) had stolen the body (John 20:2). So Peter and "the other disciple"—almost universally believed to have been the apostle John—went running to the tomb. (I note in passing that some form of the verb *run* appears often in this story. If you're accustomed to talking about the Christmas rush, let me observe that it's nothing by comparison with the Easter rush. And if perhaps we could get properly excited about Easter, we'd understand why there was so much running on the first Easter day.)

John outran Peter and got to the tomb first, but he didn't go in. Peter, always the impetuous one whether in speech or in action, went directly into the tomb. A quick survey revealed the linen wrappings and the cloth that had been on Jesus' head, carefully laid in place. Now John "also went in, and he saw and *believed*" (20:8, italics author's). This is a telling word. The Gospel writer (traditionally thought to be John himself) doesn't tell us what John believed; rather, he goes on to explain, "For as yet they did not understand the scripture, that he [Jesus] must rise from the dead" (20:9). We have no particulars about what John believed at that moment, and it's clear that John himself hadn't worked out any detailed doctrine of the Resurrection. We ascertain only that John knew there was more to the story than an empty tomb, far more than what Mary feared, that someone had stolen the body. He didn't yet understand the scripture, but he believed the miracle.

So while Mary—as we shall see in a few moments—was the first to see the resurrected Christ, John was the first to believe. These two were the first to "get" the Easter story. Mary Magdalene got it in a flesh-and-blood encounter, and John in a conviction of the heart. But each got it, and they were the first to do so.

John's story doesn't have as many dramatic possibilities as Mary's, though there is still plenty of room for reading between the lines. When Jesus called John and his brother James, they were in a small fishing business with their father, Zebedee. They left the business to follow Jesus. John came eventually to be known as the apostle of love. Tradition says that he is the only apostle who was not martyred, and that in his very old age he would be carried to a pulpit where his only message would be to "love one another."

But John didn't start that way. His early appearances in the gospel story are such that we quickly understand why Jesus referred to him and his brother James as "Sons of Thunder" (Mark 3:17). The two of them are identified as asking Jesus if they might be at his right hand and his left when he came into his kingdom (see Mark 10:35-45), with a particular insensitivity for the rest of the apostolic team. And when a Samaritan village refused hospitality to Jesus, these two volunteered that they would "command fire to come down from heaven" to destroy the village (Luke 9:51-56). And John reported proudly to Jesus that when he saw someone casting out demons in Jesus' name, he had rebuked him for doing so because the person "was not following us"—an action for which Jesus quickly corrected John (Mark 9:38-41). All of which is to say that while John didn't have seven demons, neither was he as an early disciple an admirable role model. Indeed, sometimes the subtle demons with which John was coping in those days are just as dangerous as the more terrifying ones that people saw in Mary Magdalene.

No matter. Just now I want us to remember that John was the first to believe the Easter event.

Now back to Mary Magdalene. After she had carried her news of the empty tomb to Simon Peter and John and had returned with them to the tomb, she stayed on. Peter and John "returned to their homes" (John 20:10), but "Mary stood weeping outside the tomb" (20:11). Mary simply couldn't leave. The women with whom she came to the tomb had long since left. Peter and John, who came at her insistence, also had left. But Mary couldn't leave.

Mind you, it wasn't faith that kept her at the tomb. At that point, faith seemed not to have asserted itself at all. She was staying because she felt she must leave her gift of love at the tomb of her Lord; she had brought spices to make his burial as loving and as dignified as possibly it could be—particularly since Jesus' dying had been so brutal and humiliating. And now the body was gone, so she couldn't complete her journey of love.

I realize that the fullness of the Holy Spirit was not enjoyed by humanity until the Day of Pentecost, but forgive me if I say that Mary Magdalene, who was once possessed by demons—fully and completely so, said the people who knew her best—was now filled with the Holy Spirit. I mean specifically that she was filled with the Spirit in the sense that the apostle Paul would later hold up as the criterion when he explained to the Christians at Corinth that the "more excellent" evidence of the Holy Spirit is the heart of love (1 Corinthians 12:31–13:13). Mary of Magdala had the Spirit of love.

She was at the tomb early, and she refused to leave it, because she loved her Lord. At that point, she had neither faith nor hope that she would ever see Jesus alive again, but she had the "greatest" of the virtues, love, and that love compelled her to come to the tomb *early, while it was still dark* (so dark, in fact, that faith and hope and reason were all extinguished, and the only light in Mary's universe was love). And when others had left the tomb, still she remained. Love wouldn't allow her to leave. And it was then that Jesus said her name, and she saw that her Lord was alive; the only sense in which his body was stolen was in the Resurrection power that had stolen it from the poor grasp of death.

That's how it was that Mary was the first person to see Jesus alive after his crucifixion, and one of the two persons to experience Easter at its beginning. It happened because of love.

This is the secret for John, too. Some say that John outran Peter in the race to the tomb because John was probably the youngest of the apostles. I respect that argument, but we have no reason to think that Simon Peter was decrepit; I venture he was still in his middle to late twenties. And in any event, Peter was not the kind of person to be outrun by anyone, anytime. The same energy that made him lead the way in every conversation drove him in all of life's ventures. John got to the tomb first because he was propelled by love. So, too, it was love that made John pause at the mouth of the tomb, hesitant to step possessively into the burial place of his Lord. And I dare to think that love caused John to step past the cold logic that said resurrection was impossible, and past the ignorance that hadn't grasped the scriptures promising that Jesus "must rise from the dead" (John 20:9).

But there is other evidence of John's love for Christ. As I said earlier, this fourth Gospel is traditionally said to have been written by the apostle John. One of John's fingerprints on the book is in the phrase that the author uses several times to refer to a particular disciple, including the story that we are reading in this chapter: "the one whom Jesus loved" (20:2; see also 21:20). A few verses later the writer tells us, "This is the disciple who is testifying to these things and has written them" (21:24). Those who love deeply long for depth of love. When John speaks of himself as "the disciple whom Jesus loved," he is witnessing also to his love for his Lord.

I suspect I should interrupt myself at this moment to confront an unfortunate issue. Now and again we come upon some book or an article in some periodical that interprets Jesus' relationship to both Mary Magdalene and the apostle John as being sexual in nature. I dare to say that this interpretation says more about the nature of our times than about what the Bible is saying. Unfortunately, our contemporary culture has become so sex-insistent that the word *love* cannot be used in connection with young people and adults without people giving it a sexual connotation. Ours will be a much better, much healthier world when we realize that while sexual relationships can be an important expression of love, there is much, much more to love than sex. It will be a very great gain in human relationships when we come once again to see that some of the deepest expressions of love and of friendship flourish without any element of sexual activity or expression.

Jesus had so many followers in the days before his crucifixion. The crowds that hailed him on the day we now call Palm Sunday were enthusiastic about him, and of course there were at least seventy persons whom Jesus ordained to represent him in addition to the twelve whom we know as the apostles. And the Scriptures tell us that there were a number of women who helped support the work of Jesus and the apostles, and who were present as often as possible to hear Jesus teach.

But on the morning of the first Easter, two people out of all those possible candidates experienced Easter: Mary Magdalene, in her face-to-face encounter with the risen Christ, and the apostle John, who stepped into the empty tomb *and believed.* It would be much later in the day before John would see his Lord in the flesh, but somehow he grasped that the tomb was empty not because someone had stolen Jesus' body, but because the power of death had been broken by Jesus' resurrection.

Why John and Mary Magdalene, out of the several hundred who might have been the first? I believe it was because of their love—love that made Mary come early and stay late, and love that made John run to the tomb, then step back in reverence, then grasp something that he himself couldn't explain: that Jesus had been raised from the dead.

If we are to get to the heart of the Easter story and the Easter experience, we need all three of the great virtues: faith, hope, and love. But love has a place of its own. When Mary Magdalene was utterly without hope, love compelled her to stay at the place where Jesus had been buried. And when John looked at the empty tomb and *believed,* I insist that his faith was born in his love. Mind you, I'm not saying that Peter or the women who came with Mary Magdalene didn't love Jesus; I'm only saying what all of us know, that love shows itself in varying degrees.

And I want to say another word. I believe that in literally thousands of instances, people who could not be convinced of the Resurrection by logic or argument have grasped it because of love. Losing someone they've loved dearly, they have fumbled in the darkness of their loneliness, wishing they could believe. And love has opened the door that logic could not. Easter, you see, is a love story.

CHAPTER 6

Late for Easter

1 CORINTHIANS 15:1-11: Now I would remind you, brothers and sisters, of the good news that I proclaimed to you, which you in turn received, in which also you stand, through which also you are being saved, if you hold firmly to the message that I proclaimed to you—unless you have come to believe in vain.

For I handed on to you as of first importance what I in turn had received: that Christ died for our sins in accordance with the scriptures, and that he was buried, and that he was raised on the third day in accordance with the scriptures, and that he appeared to Cephas, then to the twelve. Then he appeared to more than five hundred brothers and sisters at one time, most of whom are still alive, though some have died. Then he appeared to James, then to all the apostles. Last of all, as to one untimely born, he appeared also to me. For I am the least of the apostles, unfit to be called an apostle, because I persecuted the church of God. But by the grace of God I am what I am, and his grace toward me has not been in vain. On the contrary, I worked harder than any of them—though it was not I, but the grace of God that is with me. Whether then it was I or they, so we proclaim and so you have come to believe.

*A*n adjective has been added to the name of the apostle Thomas, and it has become so much a part of his name that many people never mention his name without the adjective: *doubting. Doubting Thomas.*

I've used the term myself, both in sermons and in print. But I've come to feel that it isn't the best descriptive term for this sometimes maligned man, because in truth he wasn't necessarily questioning the idea of a resurrection or the power of God to do such a deed; rather, he was questioning the perceptive abilities of his colleagues, and perhaps also their ability to distinguish facts from hopes and dreams. I think the better word for Thomas is *late*. His whole problem came with his being absent on the evening of the first Easter. If he had been present that evening when Jesus appeared to the rest of the apostles, he never would have had reason to doubt their story. But as the Gospel of John reports the events, "Thomas (who was called the Twin), one of the twelve, was not with them when Jesus came" (John 20:24). I think if I were to be a pastor again, I might make the phrase "Remember Thomas" the closing word in letters to my congregation and the final word on each Sunday's bulletin. You never know what might happen the next time God's people come together, so you'd better be there. Otherwise you'll be a latecomer, like Thomas; or worse, never get to the point at all.

But there was someone who experienced Easter later than Thomas. Much later. So late that some people didn't think he was qualified to be called an apostle. I am referring to that person whom many consider the greatest of the apostles, the man of Tarsus named Saul, who is revered among us now as the apostle Paul.

Paul is thoroughly candid about his story. As he lists the numbers of persons who saw the resurrected Christ, he comes finally to himself: "*Last of all*, as to one untimely born, he appeared also to me. For I am the least of the apostles, unfit to be called an apostle, because I persecuted the church of God" (1 Corinthians 15:8-9, italics author's).

When Paul includes his name among those who experienced Easter, he gives us no details. We can be quite sure, however, that he is not referring to an appearance of Christ during the days between the Resurrection and the Ascension.

Paul makes that clear when he describes himself as "one untimely born." He didn't come into the scene "on time" as did the other apostles. And we could also note that if he had seen the risen Christ during those weeks when Jesus appeared and reappeared in visits with the apostles and other believers, he never would have launched his campaign to wipe out the followers of Jesus and their message. He would, rather, have become a convert at that moment or very soon thereafter.

But although Paul came to Easter late, I dare to say that no one was ever more thoroughly convinced of the Easter event, and no one ever articulated the story more eloquently and effectively than this man, Saul of Tarsus.

As his name indicates, Saul was from the city of Tarsus, one of the major cities of its time. He came from a family of some substance, as indicated by the fact that they possessed Roman citizenship, a status much prized and not easily obtained. His family also provided him with the advantage of a superior education, through study with a Jewish scholar, Gamaliel. And it is obvious that Saul's family had a deep sense of their Jewish heritage, and that they conveyed this pride and commitment to their son.

Privileges and advantages make some people lazy and self-satisfied. Not Saul. He was ambitious—and perhaps it could be said, ambitious in the highest sense. That is, he set his eyes on the most admirable goal, a life of religious excellence. He won acceptance to the group known as Pharisees, probably the most demanding body within Judaism. So when a body appeared within Judaism that followed a teacher from Galilee, Jesus of Nazareth, Saul quickly allied himself with a group of his spiritual elders who dedicated themselves to wiping out the movement. Our first sight of Saul is on the occasion when a young follower of Jesus was being stoned to death because of his faith. Those leading the charge laid their garments at Saul's feet. The biblical author reports somewhat laconically, "And Saul approved of their killing him" (Acts 8:1).

Such an event would unnerve many people, perhaps to the

point where they would begin examining their convictions and motivations. It was quite the opposite with Saul. He responded like a wild creature that has had its first taste of blood. As loving friends buried the body of the martyr, Stephen, young Saul set about "ravaging the church by entering house after house; dragging off both men and women," so he could commit them to prison (Acts 8:3). There's something frightening about a person so intent on wiping out a movement that he would break into homes and apprehend (the writer of Acts uses a more violent word, "dragging") both men and women simply because of what they believed. I suspect this lets us know the power this man saw in what people believe. For him, beliefs were no casual matter; they contained the power of revolution, for good or ill—and Saul saw only ill in what these people believed.

So it was, until a day when Saul himself was apprehended by the very one whose followers he had been seeking so furiously to destroy. And with that, Saul the persecutor became Saul the convert; and in time, Paul the apostle.

Twenty or thirty years passed by, in which Paul went passionately from city to city, witnessing to the faith he had once decried. At first he did so as an assistant to a great soul named Barnabas, but then he himself became the leader, assisted by a variety of younger preachers and teachers. He felt compelled in time to concentrate on the people whom formerly he had been most inclined to despise, Gentiles.

Some twenty or twenty-five years after his conversion, Paul preached in the city of Corinth, which was a center both of commerce and of vice. His converts came from a wide swath of humanity, most of it morally marginal at best. But the gospel worked for them just as it had for Paul, and before long there was a thriving church in Corinth, like an island of hope in a sea of corruption. A major element in Paul's preaching—as with all of the first generation of Christian preachers—was the good news of Easter: that Jesus Christ had been victorious over death and the grave, with a power that had conquered death for all who would follow Jesus.

Paul moved on from Corinth to plant more churches throughout Asia Minor and what is now Europe. But before long, bad news came from Corinth—a plethora of problems and questions. One of the most devastating was that some false teacher had convinced many of the young believers that there wasn't really a resurrection from the dead. So Paul set out to answer the questions this heresy had raised. In the process he has left us the most sustained discussion of the Resurrection in the New Testament.

Paul begins by reminding the Corinthians that what he had delivered to them was *good news*, and that it was in this message that they should *stand*. He outlines the basics: that Christ died for our sins, that he was buried, then raised from the dead on the third day—all of this "in accordance with the scriptures" (1 Corinthians 15:3-4). Paul then lists a number of the occasions when Christ appeared to his followers after his resurrection, including an occasion not mentioned elsewhere in the New Testament, when "he appeared to more than five hundred brothers and sisters at one time, most of whom are still alive, though some have died" (15:6), though he doesn't mention the key, early appearance to Mary Magdalene (see John 20:1-18).

Paul reminds the people that if there is no resurrection of the dead, as some were saying, then neither was Christ raised from the dead—in which case, "your faith is futile and you are still in your sins" (1 Corinthians 15:17). That is, the whole Christian enterprise rests upon the fact of our Lord's resurrection. Paul then charges forward with reassurance: "But in fact Christ has been raised from the dead"; and in his rising, he became "the first fruits of those who have died" (15:20). That is, Jesus' resurrection was the beginning of an endless harvest of life, with every believer to the end of time being part of that grand collection.

Paul then proceeds to answer the everyday questions that we humans are inclined to raise. They're the sorts of questions that we bring up in small-group discussions or perhaps in a private meeting in the pastor's study—questions that seem trivial, perhaps even foolish, but that bother us; questions such as, "How are the dead raised? With what kind of body do they come?" (15:35). Paul's answers sometimes seem a bit impatient, but in any event he gives the answers. And in the process he unfolds something of the doctrines of sin and of salvation. He explains, "The first man, Adam, became a living being; the last Adam [that is, Jesus Christ] became a lifegiving spirit" (15:45). The apostle takes us back to the Creation scene: "The first man was from the earth, a man of dust; the second man is from heaven" (15:47). Obviously we humans have our tie with the "man of dust," because we "are of the dust"; but Paul wants us to know that now through Christ, we are just as surely "those who are of heaven"(15:48).

It is very simple and very logical as Paul sees it: "Just as we have borne the image of the man of dust, we will also bear the image of the man of heaven" (15:49). To put it another way (reflecting our Lord's conversation with Nicodemus [see John 3:1-10]), our creation origins are from the dust of the earth (see Genesis 2:7), but our new creation is from the spirit of God, through our new birth in Jesus Christ. This new birth prepares us—makes us eligible, so to speak—for the resurrection, because in the new birth the Holy Spirit takes control. This control will reach its climax when the body, too, is translated into a heavenly body. This is the faith that we Christians declare each time we recite the Apostles' Creed: "I believe in . . . the resurrection of the body."

Then Paul speaks both as pastor and as herald. In the warmth of faith, he addresses the people at Corinth (who often disappoint him and clearly at times irritate him), "What I am saying, brothers and sisters, is this: flesh and blood cannot inherit the kingdom of God, nor does the perishable inherit the imperishable." But the time is coming when "the dead will be raised imperishable, and we will be changed. For this perishable body must put on imperishability, and this mortal body must put on immortality." When that happens, it can finally be said, "Death has been swallowed up in victory" (1 Corinthians 15:50-54). As Paul promised at the outset, this is *good news.* I dare say, in fact, that it is the best news our human race has ever heard, and Paul wants to be sure that it isn't lost.

Paul is especially anxious that we should get the connection between the first Easter morning and our own human experience. So it is that Paul explains that he teaches as he does "because we know that the one who raised the Lord Jesus will raise us also with Jesus" (2 Corinthians 4:14). And when Paul wants to encourage the believers in Rome to live in the Spirit—that is, in a manner pleasing to God—he makes his case by reminding them that they are a resurrection people. "If the Spirit of him who raised Jesus from the dead dwells in you, he who raised Christ from the dead will give life to your mortal bodies also through his Spirit that dwells in you" (Romans 8:11). Easter is not simply a holiday to be celebrated with church attendance and a festive dinner; it is a new power let loose in our world that enables us—to the degree that we are willing—to live a new kind of life. Why? Because the very power that raised Christ from the dead now dwells in us.

All of which is to say that Paul has a particularly commanding grasp on the Easter story. He is moved by it more deeply, explains it more carefully, and seems to understand the implications of its power more profoundly than any other New Testament writer. Yet he was a latecomer to Easter. He wasn't present on that first morning, as were Mary Magdalene and John and Simon Peter, or that evening when our Lord entered the meeting room where the doors were closed, or at the later gathering where Thomas's challenge was answered. We have to conclude also that he wasn't among that larger group of five hundred who saw Jesus at another time, else when he mentioned this group surely he would have identified himself as being among their number.

So when did Paul see his risen Lord? The only hint we have—and in my mind, it is a substantial hint, if not an outright declaration—was at the time of his conversion. Saul, as he was then known, was on his way to Damascus, intent on the brutal work to which he had committed himself, "still breathing threats and murder against the disciples of the Lord" (Acts 9:1), empowered for his assignment with letters from the high priest. If he found any followers of Jesus, men or women, he intended to bind them and bring them to Jerusalem for trial.

As he approached Damascus with his companions, "a light from heaven flashed around him" (9:3). He heard a voice as he fell to the ground: "Saul, Saul, why do you persecute me?" Saul was a devout man, however misled he might have been, and he recognized that the voice was more than human. He asked, "Who are you, Lord?" And the voice answered, "I am Jesus, whom you are persecuting" (9:4-5).

In the flash of light, Saul lost his sight. Now the leader became the led. His associates took him into Damascus, where he remained without sight for three days, in which time he neither ate nor drank. Those had to have been days of intense soul-searching. I notice an interesting detail, as perhaps you have, too. It isn't significant enough to build a doctrine, but as I've said, it's interesting: Saul suffered three days of blindness, just as our Lord was in the tomb for parts of three days. Those days were entombment days for Saul: his past was lying shattered around him, while he waited for the wonder of new life.

Well, you probably know the rest of Saul's story: how he became, in time, the prince of the apostles, born out of due time as he said, but with a passion for Christ and for faith that caused him to surpass all those who had come to know Christ before him. Beginning, through the gracious invitation of Barnabas, to work as Barnabas's assistant, Paul soon became the leader of their little team, and eventually he became the one who pioneered the introduction of the gospel to the continent of Europe.

With it all, Paul became the most articulate messenger of the Resurrection, the greatest Easter preacher of the first century—and the source of ten millions of Easter sermons in the nearly twenty centuries since then.

And here's the marvel of it all: Paul was late for Easter. While Mary Magdalene and her friends were coming to the tomb, and while Peter, John, James, Thomas, and hundreds of others were seeing Christ face-to-face in the weeks following his resurrection, Paul was an angry soul, wondering how he could stamp out this new faith movement.

But then he met the resurrected Christ—met him in his own conversion. Met him, that is, in the same way you and I are privileged to meet Christ in this twenty-first century, by acknowledging him as our Lord and by choosing to follow him as earnestly as we can.

I feel very close to Paul—for my sake and for yours. Because he was late for Easter, just as we are; after all, everyone couldn't live in the first century. But he came to know Christ through the power that was let loose in our world by the Resurrection. And by the fruits of his life, Paul proved that meeting the Christ of Easter by faith can be just as life-transforming and life-giving as meeting him in an upper room or on the road to Emmaus. That's part of the message of Easter: that Jesus Christ is so alive, so real, and so present that we can know him today as certainly as John and Mary Magdalene knew him on the first of all Easters.

CHAPTER 7

Forever Easter

REVELATION 21:1-4: Then I saw a new heaven and a new earth; for the first heaven and the first earth had passed away, and the sea was no more. And I saw the holy city, the new Jerusalem, coming down out of heaven from God, prepared as a bride adorned for her husband. And I heard a loud voice from the throne saying,
"See, the home of God is among mortals.

He will dwell with them as their God;
they will be his peoples,
and God himself will be with them;
he will wipe every tear from their eyes.
Death will be no more;
mourning and crying and pain will be no more,
for the first things have passed away."

*E*aster is the beginning of a story, not the end. It is a climax, yes—one can hardly imagine a more dramatic climax than this one, when the angel announces, "Why do you look for the living among the dead? He is not here, but has risen" (Luke 24:5). The only reason this doesn't shake and startle us is that we've heard it so often in ritual and sermon and song that we don't *really* hear it. But if we did, the dramatist in us might reason that this is the signal for a curtain to be dropped on our human drama. After all, if death, the last enemy, has been defeated, what more is there to say? Instead, however, a new curtain opens before us, leading us into a scene that is quite beyond anything we had previously been able to envision.

Still and all, in a sense what we're about to discuss is not a new story but the picking up of the plot of an old story—a story so old that we're surprised that it hasn't been forgotten. Indeed, it probably would have been forgotten except that something about it seems to have been written into our spiritual genetic code from farther back than conscious memory can construct. How long has it been, I wonder, since we humans began to hope, to believe—indeed, to *insist*—that there must be more to this life of ours than the years we get on this earth? How is it that we dare to think that "earth to earth, ashes to ashes, dust to dust" simply must be followed by, "in sure and certain hope of resurrection to eternal life, through our Lord Jesus Christ"? Where was it planted in our human psyche that there is something in us of too much worth to be snuffed out with some poor, last gasp?

If you want my opinion (and since you're reading this book, you're compelled for a moment at least to hear it), I believe that this conviction is as old as Eden. I'm taking you back to the chapter that opened our time together. You will remember that somewhere beyond our best records, beyond anything science can effectively articulate, ours was an idyllic scene. Everything about this planet and the universe surrounding it was just right, just perfect, just Edenic, to use a biblical sort of word. And that's what we lost when we humans began making choices that separated us from God and love and goodness and justice—and in the process, separated us from life.

Well, this might make you feel that God lost control of the human story. And as a matter of fact, it has been a pretty up-and-down account since then, a kind of five losses for every six gains, it sometimes seems—and sometimes as you get the evening news, you have a feeling that the score is in fact going the other way.

But don't you believe it. Although human sin is a power-ful, destructive force, God's plan cannot finally and com-pletely be destroyed by it. Indeed, in the end our sin cannot in any way diminish God's ultimate purposes. Which is to say that as we follow the Easter story on into eternity (there's a key word), we begin to realize that God doesn't simply restore our world to what it once was; God makes it better than the original. God does so by investing his Son in the enterprise, so that what we get is not just a return to Eden, but what the Bible describes as a new heaven and a new earth.

Let me interrupt myself for a moment to sermonize. I promise not to be long. So often when we do something morally or ethically stupid (that is, something *wrong* and *sin-ful*, which is the worst form of stupidity), we get the sad feel-ing that life can never be the same again. Some of our words and deeds are bad enough to justify such a feeling of hope-lessness. So hear me: it may indeed be true that because of what we have done, or because of what someone else has done to us, life can never be the same again. But by the grace of God, it can be better. There is nothing in my badness that is greater than God's goodness. Mind you, we may suffer a great deal because of our sins, and we may experience great physical, emotional, and spiritual loss, and bring great pain and loss to others. But these need not be the end of the story. Easter is at work in our world even now, every day, in the midst of our still-imperfect world. So God can—and will, if we want it—lead us not simply to a restoration of the past, but to some-thing better: a new heaven and a new earth even now. This is part of that wonderful idea called *grace*. We ought to give it more of a chance in our daily lives and in the lives of others. Sometimes, indeed, we might allow ourselves to be agents of grace in the life of somebody who is currently wrestling with hopelessness and brokenness.

But back to our story. The first believers, eyewitnesses as most of them were to the teaching and miracles of Jesus, had a wealth of material from which to preach. If they wanted, they could relate almost endless stories of the healings they had seen Jesus perform, or of his confrontations with the Pharisees, and they could recite some of his special stories and themes nearly word for word. No doubt the early apostolic sermons contained a good deal of that kind of material, along with the sort of supporting background from the Hebrew Scriptures that meant so much to those early converts, most of whom had their spiritual roots in Judaism. But it is quite clear in the sermons and witnesses that come to us in the book of Acts that one theme stood out above all others—the resurrection of Jesus. For the first Christians, Jesus' resurrection was the foundation for everything that they believed. Thus at the Day of Pentecost, Peter explained to the crowd this new working of God in their midst by pointing them to what had just happened, "This Jesus God raised up, and of that all of us are witnesses," and he built his case on a reference to the words of David in the book of Psalms (Acts 2:32-35). Not long thereafter, after Peter and John had healed "a man lame from birth" at the gate of the temple (Acts 3:1-10), Peter charged the crowd with having "killed the Author of life, whom God raised from the dead" (Acts 3:15). Then, when the religious authorities asked the apostles under what authority and by what name they had healed this beggar, Peter answered that it was "by the name of Jesus Christ of Nazareth, whom you crucified, whom God raised from the dead" (Acts 4:10).

And the crucial significance of the Resurrection didn't diminish in any way as that first generation of believers and preachers led the way into a second generation. Indeed, if anything, the witness became still more emphatic. So the apostle Paul gave a shattering dimension to the Resurrection when he wrote, "If Christ has not been raised, your faith is futile and you are still in your sins" (1 Corinthians 15:17). That is, for the first generation of Christians, nothing mattered more than the Easter story. Paul declared that he preached "Christ, and him crucified" (1 Corinthians 2:2), but as already indicated, the Crucifixion itself became meaningless if it was not followed by the Easter event. The death of Christ and his resurrection were not an end in themselves, but signs pointing to a new, universal fact, that the power of sin and death had been broken through Jesus' death and resurrection.

The book of Revelation was written in the last decade of the first century, roughly two generations after the first Easter. The times were not good for those who had chosen to follow Jesus of Nazareth. Like the Jews, Jesus' followers were of course seen askance by the Roman Empire because they insisted that there was only one God and therefore they could not worship Caesar. There was a kind of religious freedom in the empire: all religions were tolerated as long as their adherents were also willing to bow down to the emperor, but since Jews and Christians would not do that, they were always open to persecution from the government. The odds were increased for the Christians, however, because their numbers were growing so rapidly. All over the Roman Empire (and indeed, beyond its political boundaries), believers were winning still other believers, all of which made the government increasingly uneasy with this grassroots movement, so there were sporadic and sometimes gruesomely violent periods of persecution.

It was at such a time that the Revelation was written. The author—traditionally seen as the apostle John—was himself banished to "the island called Patmos because of the word of God and the testimony of Jesus"; so it was that he would write to his fellow believers that he shared with them in "the persecution and the kingdom and the patient endurance" (Revelation 1:9). The times were of a kind that most of us cannot really imagine. We hear of such circumstances in reports from believers who live in places where to be a Christian is to put one's life in daily peril—where gathering to worship is an exercise in courage, or where a knock on the door (or a boot against the door) may mean that some family member, or perhaps the whole family, will be carried off to a sham trial or simply to imprisonment, punishment, and probably death. I repeat, we can hardly imagine such a world, but such it is for millions in our day, and such it was for the people who first got the Revelation that John received from our Lord.

At its heart the book of Revelation is a resurrection message, a report on how wide and deep and high Easter reaches. Because of course none of the ultimate triumphs over evil would be possible if it were not for the death of our Lord on Calvary and the Resurrection that followed on the third day.

Revelation unfolds on a vast canvas. Not only does it report on a planetwide, historical level; it takes us into the dimensions of heaven and hell, and of those spiritual forces that influence human history for good and ill. Some of the battle descriptions in Revelation are monstrous and grotesque. The writer uses such language and imagery because there is no other way to convey to us the utter ugliness of sin and what it has done not only to our individual lives but also to politics, economics, and the living out of history through the ages. Defeating such evil begins with God's supreme act of love, in the sacrifice of his Son. Thus when the audience of eternity waits for someone to open the denouement of all things, the only one in the universe worthy to do so is "a Lamb standing as if it had been slaughtered" (Revelation 5:1-6).

But when the story comes to its consummation in the closing chapters of Revelation, we enter a scene as tranquil and beautiful as some earlier chapters were horrific. We behold "a new heaven and a new earth; for the first heaven and the first earth had passed away" (Revelation 21:1). As we read this report, we recall that in the Genesis report of Creation, everything about the "first" heaven and earth was so perfect that God could express divine satisfaction with each step in the process.

But now we need something infinitely better. The first earth had gone awry through the choices made by our human race, so now, as the writer of Revelation sees it, we need a whole new system. I won't venture to say whether this passage is to be interpreted figuratively or literally; I'm satisfied, however, to say that this new setting is better than the original. I speak this out of my confidence in the very nature of God. As I said earlier, evil is never so great as to diminish God's work or God's purposes. Rather, God takes the stuff of our human sins and errors and builds on them a structure of greater glory and beauty than the original.

How beautiful? John is compelled to use human measures and figures of speech, since this is all he has to work with and it is also all that we can comprehend. He tells us that this new creation is "as a bride adorned for her husband" (21:2). I hope I do not sound sexist when I suggest that there could hardly be a lovelier and more encompassing figure of speech. The term implies not only physical beauty but also the spiritual beauty of love—love both in the bride's beauty and in the companion's ability to see the beauty that is presented.

Now John gives us more detail. "See, the home of God is among mortals. / He will dwell with them; / they will be his peoples, / and God himself will be with them" (21:3). The communion that was violated by sin in Eden is now—as I see it—even better than in Eden. Because where the human ability to commune with God before the Fall was a communion by nature, the people who now commune with God are those who commune by choice. They—we—are the fruit of the struggle to be the people of God, a body of persons who by the constant process of choice have made Christ the Lord of our lives.

With all of this, however, one strategic point must be reinforced. John is writing for folks like you and me—for those who have seen death at work and who have known the tears that can come in any harsh day when some presentiment of death mars the loveliness of life. So he goes to the heart of the matter. God, he tells us, "will wipe every tear from their eyes. / Death will be no more; / mourning and crying and pain will be no more, / for the first things have passed away" (21:4). Now we see an additional pragmatic reason why we needed "a new heaven and a new earth"—because the old creation had about it too much of the residue of paradise lost; we need now a place where the stuff of loss—tears, death, mourning, crying, pain—is gone, and where it can never find lodging again.

And in case we've missed the point, the one "seated on the throne" underlines what has happened: "*See, I am making all things new*" (21:5, italics author's). This is the land of Easter Forever.

But what does this have to do with our here and now?

For one thing, it is a word of sublime hope. It reminds us that this world of ours is headed toward a magnificent destination. Sometimes the pattern of history—especially as seen up close in the late-night news—seems to suggest that our world has no sure destination. Or if it does, that the destination is perverse and absurd. We need to remind ourselves, as often as possible, that God intends that in time, "all things [will be] new."

And there's another word, too, a word from the apostle Paul—a no-nonsense kind of word, even though a very wonderful one. The apostle explains that we who believe in Christ receive the benefits of his death and resurrection. And then, the challenge: "So if you have been raised with Christ, seek the things that are above, where Christ is, seated at the right hand of God. Set your minds on things that are above, not on things that are on earth" (Colossians 3:1-2). To put it clearly, Paul is telling us that if we believe in Easter, we ought to live like it. The endless Easter has not yet come, and we are not yet in that sublime city. But it is our privilege—indeed, our challenge—to take hold of as much of the Easter life as we can claim in this present world.

Because the power of death was broken some two millennia ago, our human story is headed toward Easter Forever. But meanwhile, God calls us to celebrate Easter now, every day, by living as those who "have been raised with Christ." Why would we want to settle for less?

Easter from the Back Side

JOHN D. SCHROEDER

In this book, author J. Ellsworth Kalas approaches the biblical Easter story in a new way by looking beyond the traditional Gospel scriptures to connect the story of Christ's resurrection with other stories and scriptures throughout the Bible. To assist you in facilitating a beneficial study for both you and members of your group, here are some thoughts on how you can help your group:

1. Distribute the book to participants before your first meeting and request that they come having read the first chapter. You may want to limit the size of your group to increase participation.
2. Begin your sessions on time. Your participants will appreciate your promptness. You may wish to begin your first session with introductions and a brief get-acquainted time. Start each session by reading aloud the snapshot summary of the chapter.

3. Select discussion questions and activities in advance. Note that the first question usually is a general question designed to get discussion going. The last question often is designed to summarize the discussion. Feel free to change the order of the listed questions and to create your own questions. Allow a set amount of time for the questions and activities.

4. Remind your participants that all questions are valid as part of the learning process. Encourage their participation in discussion by saying that there are no "wrong" answers and that all input will be appreciated. Invite participants to share their thoughts, personal stories, and ideas as their comfort level allows.

5. Some questions may be more difficult to answer than others. If you ask a question and no one responds, begin the discussion by venturing an answer yourself. Then ask for comments and other answers. Remember that some questions may have multiple answers.

6. Ask the question "Why?" or "Why do you believe that?" to help continue a discussion and give it greater depth.

7. Give everyone a chance to talk. Keep the conversation moving. Occasionally you may want to direct a question to a specific person who has been quiet. "Do you have anything to add?" is a good follow-up question to ask another person. If the topic of conversation gets off track, move ahead by asking the next question in your study guide.

8. Before moving from questions to activities, ask group members if they have any questions that have not been answered. Remember that as a leader, you do not have to know all the answers. Some answers may come from group members.

Other answers may even need a bit of research. Your job is to keep the discussion moving and to encourage participation.

9. Review the activity in advance. Feel free to modify it or to create your own activity. Encourage participants to try the "At home" activity.

10. Following the conclusion of the activity, close with a brief prayer, praying either the printed prayer from the study guide or a prayer of your own. If your group desires, pause for individual prayer petitions.

11. Be grateful and supportive. Thank group members for their ideas and participation.

12. You are not expected to be a "perfect" leader. Just do the best you can by focusing on the participants and the lesson. God will help you lead this group.

13. Enjoy your time together!

SUGGESTIONS FOR PARTICIPANTS

1. What you will receive from this study will be in direct proportion to your involvement. Be an active participant!

2. Please make it a point to attend all sessions and to arrive on time so that you can receive the greatest benefit.

3. Read the chapter and review the study guide questions prior to the meeting. You may want to jot down questions you have from the reading and also answers to some of the study guide questions.

4. Be supportive and appreciative of your group leader as well as the other members of your group. You are on a journey together.

5. Your participation is encouraged. Feel free to share your thoughts about the material being discussed.

6. Pray for your group and your leader.

Chapter 1
Why We Need Easter

SNAPSHOT SUMMARY

This chapter shows how the need for Easter began with Adam and Eve in the Garden of Eden.

REFLECTION / DISCUSSION QUESTIONS

1. What are the benefits of exploring the meaning of Easter within a small group?
2. What is the connection between Adam and Eve, and Easter?
3. Name some of the consequences of sin that resulted in a need for Easter.
4. Why can't we escape thinking about death and dying?
5. How has your view of death changed over the years?
6. Share a time when you first experienced the death of a loved one.
7. Reflect on / discuss the reasons why Easter is celebrated as a victory.
8. What does Easter tell us about God?
9. Name some of the reasons why we need Easter.
10. What additional insights or questions from this chapter would you like to explore?

ACTIVITIES

As a group: Share with your group why you look forward to Easter, and how you hope to add to the experience through your participation in this group.

At home: Reflect on past Easter experiences and celebrations. Think about the importance of Easter and the hope it provides.

Prayer: *Dear God, thank you for the gift of Easter and for what Jesus did for all of us out of your love. Help us cherish this special time of year and hold it in our hearts when we are in need of hope. Amen.*

Chapter 2
Easter from an Ash Heap

SNAPSHOT SUMMARY

This chapter explores the circumstances of Job and how, in his troubles, he sees a ray of hope and a glimpse of Easter victory.

REFLECTION / DISCUSSION QUESTIONS

1. Share a time when you felt hopeless and needed an Easter moment of hope.
2. Reflect on / discuss the life of Job before his world crashed.
3. What are some of the ways in which Job suffered?
4. How did Job react to his situation?
5. Reflect on / discuss how Job's friends tried to help him. What advice did they give to him?
6. Describe the Easter vision of Job and how it applies to us today.
7. In what ways does a "depth of lostness," such as that of Job, invite an Easter experience?
8. How does the story of Job help you view Easter from the back side?
9. Name some lessons we can learn from the life of Job.
10. What additional insights or questions from this chapter would you like to explore?

ACTIVITIES

As a group: Use newspapers, magazines, and other print or online resources to locate stories of troubled persons, like Job, in need of the kind of hope Easter brings. Share your findings

Or think about the following question: What does hope look like? Draw a symbol or an illustration of what hope means to you, and explain to the group the meaning behind your creation.

At home: Look for an opportunity to provide hope to someone who needs it. Offer a word of encouragement or a listening ear.

Prayer: *Dear God, thank you for always being there, offering hope and your love during our darkest hours. Help us pass on your love and hope to others. Amen.*

Chapter 3
Easter for the Disillusioned

SNAPSHOT SUMMARY

This chapter examines verses from the book of Ecclesiastes, the biblical author's search for hope and meaning, and how he saw Easter from the back side.

REFLECTION / DISCUSSION QUESTIONS

1. Share your own view of the book of Ecclesiastes. How do you feel about the author of Ecclesiastes and what he is trying to say?

2. When the author of Ecclesiastes writes "All is vanity," what is he really saying?
3. What is known about the author of Ecclesiastes? What clues are found in his writings?
4. Name some of the biblical author's reasons for being disillusioned.
5. How or why does the author of Ecclesiastes struggle with the issue of injustice?
6. In what ways is the author of Ecclesiastes like many people today? What makes people feel the way he felt?
7. Share a time in your life when you felt frustration or disillusionment.
8. Explain how the book of Ecclesiastes is a look at Easter from the back side.
9. How did this chapter help you look at Easter from the back side?
10. What additional insights or questions from this chapter would you like to explore?

ACTIVITIES

As a group: Assume the role of physicians; how would you cure disillusionment? Share remedies to heal frustration and to restore hope to those in need.

At home: Reflect on your own search for hope and meaning. How does your faith in Christ strengthen you?

Prayer: *Dear God, thank you for being there in times of frustration and disillusionment, when we need your hope and love. Show us how to minister to the disillusioned and to show them the promise of Easter. Amen.*

Chapter 4
Ezekiel Celebrates Easter

SNAPSHOT SUMMARY

This chapter looks at the ministry of Ezekiel and his vision of a valley of bones coming to life through the power of God.

REFLECTION / DISCUSSION QUESTIONS

1. Name some difficult or challenging times in the history of your nation.
2. How do citizens of a nation feel in times of trouble?
3. What qualifies of Ezekiel do you admire?
4. Reflect on / discuss the challenges faced by the nation of Judah during the time of Ezekiel.
5. Describe the experience of Ezekiel in the valley of dry bones. What was God trying to communicate to him and to us today?
6. What is significant about the bones in the valley being very dry?
7. How was this experience a preview of Easter for Ezekiel?
8. Reflect on / discuss some cures for "dry bones"— times or occasions when a person lacks life and hope.
9. How does the story of Ezekiel help you better understand Easter?
10. What additional insights or questions from this chapter would you like to explore?

ACTIVITIES

As a group: Discuss: How was Ezekiel's "valley of bones" both like and unlike a cemetery? What are some of the different feelings people may have when they visit a cemetery? What messages or images of hope do you see there? Share a related personal experience, if you desire.

At home: Use your Bible to review the story of Ezekiel and seek additional insights into life, death, hope, and Easter.

Prayer: *Dear God, thank you for reminding us of your power and promise to bring dry bones to life. Be with us during the difficult times in life, and help us always to have hope in you. Amen.*

Chapter 5
Easter Is a Love Story

SNAPSHOT SUMMARY

This chapter examines the love and faith of Mary Magdalene and the disciple John on the first Easter morning.

REFLECTION / DISCUSSION QUESTIONS

1. Share your first memory of hearing the Easter story, or a time in your life when the Easter story became very real.
2. Reflect on / discuss what is known about Mary Magdalene.
3. What does the Easter story tell us about the power of love?
4. Share a time when you experienced love's power.

5. Describe John's experience at the tomb and how he must have felt.
6. Why did Mary refuse to leave the tomb?
7. What do you admire most about Mary? What do you admire about John?
8. Describe some of the experiences and expressions of love that took place on that first Easter morning.
9. How did this chapter help you better understand the Easter story?
10. What additional insights or questions from this chapter would you like to explore?

ACTIVITIES

As a group: Use art supplies to create one or more Easter cards with themes of love, hope, and faith.

At home: Look for an opportunity to share God's love this week with a person in need.

Prayer: *Dear God, thank you for the testimony of Mary Magdalene and the apostle John, who experienced the joy of that first Easter. Help us to remember their examples of love and faith as we minister in your name to others. Amen.*

Chapter 6
Late for Easter

SNAPSHOT SUMMARY

This chapter shows how the apostle Paul arrived late for Easter but was one of the most articulate messengers of the Resurrection.

REFLECTION / DISCUSSION QUESTIONS

1. Share a time when the Easter experience came alive for you. Was it in church? during Easter dinner at home? or through the death of a loved one?
2. How does it feel to be a latecomer to an event or an experience?
3. Reflect on / discuss what is known about the life of Saul, before he became the apostle Paul.
4. What do you admire most about Paul, and why?
5. Describe Paul's ministry concerning his conversion. What were some of his triumphs and troubles?
6. Explain why Paul has such a commanding grasp of the Easter story.
7. How did Paul come to know the risen Christ?
8. What words would you use to describe the apostle Paul and his faith?
9. How did this chapter help you better understand Easter?
10. What additional insights or questions from this chapter would you like to explore?

ACTIVITIES

As a group: Use your Bible to locate writings or specific verses from the apostle Paul that are meaningful to you. Share how Paul's words minister to you.

At home: Reflect upon the life of Paul for further insights into living a life of faith and hope.

Prayer: *Dear God, thank you for the life and ministry of the apostle Paul. Help us remember the importance of Easter and of sharing the good news with others. Amen.*

Chapter 7
Forever Easter

SNAPSHOT SUMMARY

This chapter explores the book of Revelation and shows how it promises a Forever Easter.

REFLECTION / DISCUSSION QUESTIONS

1. What is meant by the author's first sentence, "Easter is the beginning of a story, not the end?
2. Why do many people think there must be more to life than our days on earth?
3. Reflect on / discuss what *grace* is and its Easter connection.
4. What is known about the book of Revelation and its author?
5. How did the apostle Paul give a new and "shattering" dimension to the Resurrection?
6. What is the purpose of Revelation, and how is it connected to the Easter message?
7. According to the author, "Paul is telling us that if we believe in Easter, we ought to live like it"; explore the truth in that statement.
8. What does it mean that the Easter story will go on into eternity?
9. How did this chapter help you better understand Easter from the back side?
10. What additional insights or questions from this chapter would you like to explore?

ACTIVITIES

As a group: To mark the conclusion of this small group study, hold your own Easter celebration and graduation party.

At home: Reflect upon what you gained from reading this book and participating in this small group study, and how they enhanced your Easter experience.

Prayer: *Dear God, thank you for providing all of us with new insights into the power and meaning of Easter. Thank you once again for your son, Jesus, and for what he did for all of us out of your love. Bless us and be with us as we continue our spiritual journeys. Amen.*